ANDREA MONDOUX

EMBODY
Bliss

Break Free From the Shoulds and Move Into More Joy

Contents

Reader Reviews

"Reading Embody Bliss felt like sitting down with your wisest, most vulnerable best friend, the one who tells the truth with love and swears when it matters. Andrea Mondoux has written a powerhouse of a book for any woman who's ever felt stuck in the 'shoulds' and is ready to reclaim joy, intuition, and radical self-trust. A must-read for every woman ready to trade burnout for bliss."

— Susan Hyatt, Master Certified Life Coach
   & Author of *Bare*

"Embody Bliss was such a joy, it's heartfelt, funny, and beautifully real. From the very first page, it felt like a love letter to growth: a reminder of the work we've done, the healing we're in, and the journey that still lies ahead. It's one of those books you want to keep close by your bedside, in your bag, just to remind yourself of how incredible you are. What I loved most was seeing how deeply Andrea cares for others reflected in the way she now shows up and cares for herself. Watching that shift, trusting yourself more, setting boundaries, cheering yourself on, was so moving to read."

— Chris Kufske, Founder and Photographer at
   Click Photography

"What a beautifully grounded, authentic, and relatable read this book is. I love how Andrea has incorporated her real life experiences that tie in with the strategies she shares in this easy to follow, practical guide to personal growth. Life can feel really overwhelming, and we don't often realize that we can shift how we see and move through the challenges of being human. This book will have you feeling less alone and encouraged as you take steps to improving the experience of your life, and you'll be continually supported with the tools provided as you move through your personal growth journey. This book truly is for anyone who is tired of living in struggle and wants more for themselves."

**— Christine Dainard, Founder and Coach,
It's Me Christine D**

"If I would have had a book like this growing up and or while experiencing early adulthood (so unhappy with my body) I would have absolutely had a different and more positive outlook and journey. We need more literature like this in a space that is overloaded with diet culture and how to have instant happiness from removing weight from our bodies. Andrea's book will be such a helpful and important tool to have!"

**— Zoe Potter, Canadian Lifestyle Content and
Video Creator @lovezoepotter**

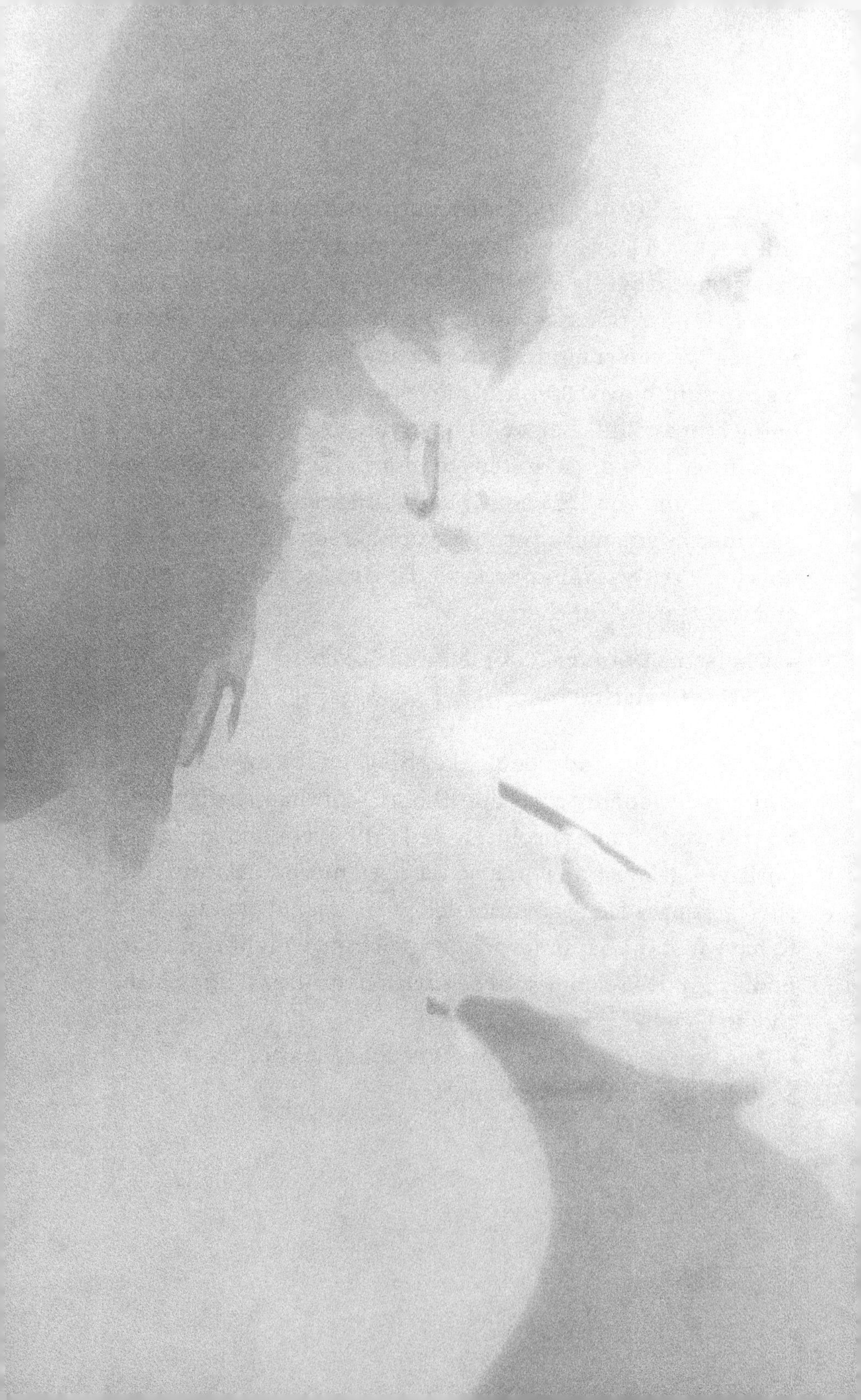

Gift For You,
Dear Reader,

I know that change doesn't happen just by reading something once, it happens through repetition, reflection, and the willingness to come back to the work again and again. That's why, alongside each chapter, I've created a companion audio integration designed to help you absorb the lessons on a deeper level.

These audios are meant to be revisited in your car, on a walk, before bed, whenever you need a reminder of who you're becoming. Our brains are wired through repetition. The more we hear a new belief or way of thinking, the more those messages carve fresh neural pathways that shape how we experience the world.

I wanted to make sure you had as many tools as possible to succeed, not just to read these words but to live them. These audio integrations are your bridge from understanding to embodiment. Take them with you. Listen often. Let them settle in.

The tools are here now, it's in your hands.

Access your FREE audio integrations

and be inspired to take action!

Dedication

Sugar and Bean, you truly are my world.

Everything I said, do, heal and feel is to show you what's possible for you. I know I deserve the world because I want you to believe you deserve the world too. Your mind is your most valuable resource, and the relationship you have with yourself is the most important connection. May you let no one have access to you who isn't holding both of those things with love and care, and remember to always hold yourself with love and care first.

INTRODUCTION

My Story

It feels really exciting to be sitting down again to write my second book. After I launched *You Actually Can Do This: Achieving a Healthy Lifestyle In Spite of Yourself*, I remember thinking to myself, "Well, that was a trip, and it was exhilarating, but I don't think I'll ever have another full book in me." As you can likely imagine, writing and then publishing a book is an extensive process. I really do mean it when I say I never thought I would have enough words to fill another book again. I figured I'd shared all I could and there wouldn't be much else to say. At 32, I foolishly thought I was finished—how naive. Gosh, at 32, life was just beginning.

And so, here I am 5 years later, opening up my laptop again to share more vulnerably with you all that I have continued to live and learn through. These last 5 years have kind of been another awakening. I have changed so much, and I felt like I could write a whole other book about it. (So I did.)

Truth is, I am so proud of that first book. 5 years ago, Andrea wrote that book as she embarked into the world of crushing the diet culture mentality for other people as she was working through it for herself. She knew she wanted to create change in the world, and she gave all the information she had to the book so that she could continue to drop seeds of living life a different way. That book, I truly believe, is a wonderful starting point for growth and evolution. (If you've not read it, you can find it on Amazon or Indigo online.) I talk often about continuing your growth as a human. I believe so strongly in the importance of consistently seeking to grow and become greater versions of yourself, and that is exactly what I have done. I like to call it being a student of yourself. We are lifelong students in that department!

Since launching that book, I continued to learn so much about embodying the person you want to become and all the tools which allow for that to be possible. I have grown and evolved and shown up in my life and with my clients differently, and that's what I am here to share with you in this book.

If you haven't guessed it by now, I am a coach. Formally known as a coach—informally known as your personal hype woman. Specifically, I am a transformation coach who helps ambitious and overwhelmed women reconnect with their power, realign with their wellness, and show up in life and business with clarity and confidence. This can mean exploring mindset, inner dialogue, and self-worth. This can mean helping women to understand the value of taking care of themselves in all the ways we should be but often aren't as a result of all the hats we wear and the conditioning we received growing up. A lot of the things I coach women on you are about to read about in these pages, so I don't want to give too much away yet … just another reason to encourage you to read on.

I have coached women from all over the world, which feels really cool to be able to share, because I have always wanted to create such an impact in this world, and seeing the transformations and revelations my clients go through is nothing short of amazing. I feel so honored every time someone chooses to invest in themselves and work with me, and I don't take that work lightly!

Like many coaches, my work was born from my own personal transformation, and if I can do 1:1 coaching, host retreats and events, and write books that help people to get to the place I am now faster than it took me—or be the person in their lives that reminds them of their importance and value and reminds them to prioritize themselves—then my work is done.

I feel so blessed every time I get to sit down to write another chapter or another book, because each time I do, I'm a different person coming to write these pages. I've always been drawn to a supporting role in life. I think that this started as a need to be liked by others (more on this later), and I learned early on that if I served them, they would like me. This has grown into a genuine part of my identity.

It started at a young age, when I was facilitating friendship conflicts in the schoolyard, when I was itching to do my babysitting course so that I could take care of other children (I mean, making a little money, never hurt either), and always wanting to play house with my cousins, even close to my pre-teen years. I was still playing because I loved the role of mother and caregiver. When I thought about what I wanted to do as a career, I knew it would be something in a helping profession, and at 18 years old, I enrolled in a Social Services Diploma program at a local college. The knowledge I gained through those 2 years was immeasurable, and it often shows up in the work I do because it truly set the foundation for the person I am today.

I will never forget that pivotal moment when I realized in order to really help others, you must also lean into helping yourself.

I turned 19 shortly after I started my first year, and as I sit back and think about how mature I thought I was back then, I realize I was still just a kid—like truly! A kid who had to grow up too quickly as the eldest sibling in a tense, conflict ridden divorced family, which turned into a home with 2 mothers. This didn't come without its fair share of challenges either.

Having same-sex parents wasn't as common in the 90s and 2000s or as accepted as it might be now, both among adults and among my peers. My eldest daughter openly talks about the inclusiveness and acceptance they learn about at school for all races, genders, etc., but when I was a kid, it wasn't like that. I will never forget how often girls warned each other not to change around me because I had a gay parent, or how often I heard comments about my family dynamic both from kids and adults. Looking back, I know those kids just didn't understand, and I can only imagine the things being discussed with them at home, but it doesn't change how damaging and ostracizing it felt for me at the time. Thank god for my best friend at the time, who also had 2 moms, because he would often stick up for me when kids got really mean. Thanks David.

I went from a two-mom home to a single-parent home as this "second mom" left our family. It completely blindsided me. I learned some things about the relationship, which left me feeling like the 10 years of the relationship we all had was nothing. I spent most of my late childhood and teen years being hyper-focused on the emotions of those around me and felt it necessary to be the sounding board for those I cared about. My life experiences and the traumas I've navigated as a result have enhanced my compassion, my empathy, my maturity. It has also elevated my insecurity and my constant need to seek belonging to my detriment—more on that in later chapters—and my sensitive nature.

In college, I remember taking a class called the Canadian Family Dynamic. In this course, we had to explore the families we grew up in and how the inter-generational psychological patterns in those families may have impacted how we show up in our everyday lives. My professor at the time was an incredibly wise woman. In fact, it's hard for me to articulate the amount of learning I received, how much I looked up to my 3 professors, and how much they shaped the person I am today. I am not sure where I would be without their guidance. This professor had an incredibly tough exterior, which always had me thinking she was so hard to read. She was very blunt, very to the point, and besides being a college professor, she also had her own counseling practice, which, as students, was something we all looked up to. We thought she really had it all, and she was intimidating as hell, but without fail we always left her class with some pretty insane "ah ha" moments, which kept us coming back for her every word.

In the Canadian Family Dynamic class, as she was explaining our assignment, I remember thinking to myself that the project was going to be easy! In the assignment, you mapped out your family, usually about 3 generations. Once you had listed the generations, then you had to dive further into what the relationships were like in previous generations and how they could have affected future generations—both on a positive level and a negative one. You also had to identify whether there was addiction or mental health present. In the therapy setting this can be a really freaking helpful tool, because along with the therapist, you can identify generational patterns of abuse, addiction, mental health, divorce, or conflict, and you can understand the relationships and experiences you have in your own life and how they might be affected by what happened in the family history—wild right? Especially because whether or not we know it, or whether or not we realize it, these things are the building blocks and foundations of how we see and show up in the world.

I figured I wouldn't have a lot to include in my diagram because in my naïve mind, our extended family was close, and despite having gone through all of this hardship, I was a relatively well-rounded young adult. Though I got into some mischief as I navigated the freedoms of growing up and tested the boundaries (as we all do as young adults), I had a strong moral compass. I hadn't really taken the time to do any exploratory work, self-discovery, or personal growth work.

Spoiler Alert: this was a wake-up call for me to actually see how many things were a part of my family patterns and relationships and how those have inadvertently affected me. Mental health, conflict and strain, divorce, and trauma. The instructor said to us in not so many words, *If you're going to help people unpack their shit, you probably should unpack your own first.* And that really stuck with me.

Just because I hadn't taken the time to explore my regular thoughts, my limiting beliefs, the relationships that I allowed to be a part of my reality, my boundaries, what I was and wasn't willing to tolerate in relationships, the things deep down that I really needed to heal from, how I spoke to myself, the way I felt about my body … Just because I hadn't given time to any of these things didn't mean they weren't the cornerstones or the blueprint, if you will, of how I was showing up in the world and that it would be reflected in how I helped and interacted with others.

Life. Changing. Moment.

It was a super powerful assignment. One that once you have done in depth, you can't just pretend you didn't learn it.

It gave me a lot of insight into dysfunctional family dynamics and the impact they can have. **Every single family, no matter who you are, has varying degrees of dysfunction within its system, both immediate and extended.** Some examples of this are avoiding conflict to keep the peace, holding children to incredibly high standards and not allowing them room to fail, parentification, belittling children, adverse childhood experiences, abuse, unacknowledged trauma, acknowledged trauma, letting Uncle Carson and Aunt Jeanie say whatever they want to hurt people and still allowing them back to all the family functions, and the list goes on …

Sometimes that dysfunction is so minimal, you barely see the effects from it, and other times it's so loud it's hard to get away from, and it ripples unhealed through generations. This dysfunction then sets the stage for who we think we are, what we believe we're worthy of, what we regularly tell ourselves, and most importantly, whether we allow ourselves to experience real pure and simple bliss.

This was my first exposure to what I call and believe to be personal growth. Prior to this, I hadn't even heard the term. I had gone to therapy as a child to help me process the massive life disruption that is a marital breakdown, which in hindsight I am so grateful to my mom for, but nowhere in those sessions did my counselor say to 10-year-old me, "Now let's do some self-discovery and anchor in some tools for personal growth." Though I now know, through all our discussions and homework, that's exactly what she was doing.

Fun fact: I kept a journal during the time that I worked with her. Her name was Nancy, and she had a beautifully welcoming clinic in her home. I still remember the feelings I got when I was there. She was an older, gentle woman with longer grey hair, and I loved going to see her. I still have that journal with my name written in the front, dated 1996.

I wrote a ton in that journal, lots of questions written by Nancy and then answers I thought about in between our sessions, or things that we worked on together.

***

June 4th, 1996

Question: Ways I have learned more about myself since seeing Nancy.

Answer: I have learned that it's not always ese in life when your parents divorce and don't want to be bac together. C is a part of our life and I can't change that.

Question: Ways I would like to see a difference in my life while seeing Nancy.

Answer: Not always asking for McDons. Don't worry so much about Dad. Don't fite about the rules. Don't complane wen it's bed time. Understand my felings.

Oct 8th, 1996

Dear Nancy,

I am so happy to have learned not to worry about such and such things. I have one more question for you why doesnt my mom want a cat in the house. I appreciate that you answered a lot of questions for me but I dont think you answered my main question why I was comming here but did you answer my question of why my parents divorced but anyway I am glad I met you and could talk to you. I love you. Andrea

***

I actually can't imagine my life now without personal growth and self-awareness. It's something I recommend for every human being to be a part of and to explore in whatever way feels right for them. It is such a vital component of the human experience.

Personal development is looking inward and focusing on ways to better yourself. Personal development increases your self-awareness, your self-esteem, your skills, and fulfills your aspirations[1]. Not only can you learn really cool shit about yourself, but it actually fulfills one of our innate needs as a social being. Abraham Maslow, who was a psychologist in the 1940's, published a tool called *Maslow's Hierarchy of Needs* to help explain human behavior and motivation. He rated all the needs and desires of humans in a pyramid style approach. At the bottom of the pyramid are our basic human desires like food, water, shelter, and safety. As we move up the pyramid, we see things like love, belonging, and relationships etc., which is why being connected to others and being a part of something is so important to us. The top need we have as human beings is for self-actualization and to reach our highest potential.[2]

This is where personal development comes in. If we are lacking true fulfillment and purpose, then we end up spending our lives feeling dull and unfulfilled. Growth needs do not stem from a lack of something but from a desire to grow as a person, and I, for one, can't imagine life without it.

Okay, Andrea, back to the story.

Trickled into different courses, over the next two years of this program, were elements of personal growth introductions and the development of self-awareness, even mindset work as we learned about how the brain and the nervous system functions in Psychology, which is something I find so fascinating and we will definitely dive into more in this book. In college, I also read my first personal development book, *The Four Agreements* by Don Miguel Ruiz. I loved the perspectives in this book so much—I have re-read it twice, and as I am writing this, I am kinda thinking I want to read it again, but I have a book to write. If you've never picked up this pocketbook of wisdom, I totally recommend it. (You're welcome.)

In his book, Ruiz introduces four mantras, or "agreements" as he calls them, that you should adopt in your life in order to achieve fulfillment. In his eyes, if you adopt these, you will live in your truest form and be the most connected to yourself. He explores how negative self-talk and patterns work, what society has forced you to believe, and a lot of other really valuable pieces of magic.

According to his work, the four agreements we should implement for ourselves are: *Be Impeccable With Your Word, Don't Make Assumptions, Don't Take Anything Personally, and Always Do Your Best.*[3] They seem so simple, and yet as I explored these components to help live a more enlightened and pleasurable life, it got me reflecting on my own thought patterns.

Reflecting on thought patterns is the basis of how I show up in the work I do with my clients today. I have learned that the tens of thousands of messages your mind sends you 24 hours a day, 7 days a week, 365 days a year, single-handedly create the reality you are experiencing. Boom. And most of us blindly follow them and believe them to be true because we were never truly taught to question what's inside our own heads. Not only that, but there is actually only a small percentage of our thoughts we are even cognitively aware of.

Did you know that your conscious mind makes up less than 10 percent of your total brain function, which means the subconscious mind represents around 90 percent.[4] The subconscious mind is often an extensive collection of unintentional habitual thoughts, behaviors, and actions.

So basically, unless we're actively exploring what our minds are saying to us—or someone like me tells you to—there will come a day when we reach the end of our life journey, still be believing all the stories we have been sold and told from the world and the people around us without consideration that perhaps some of these thoughts we're having are not our own, and are in fact, not serving us at all.

Let me say that again. I would bet (a whole lot!) that there are thoughts going through your mind at this very moment—go ahead, take a pause and think about this—that were planted by something or someone around you. And, because it's coming from within, you believe it as truth. Don't think about that too much yet, it gets overwhelming, trust me.

I have some good news for you though. We're going to work through this together through the power of thought work in the first chapter!

Before I get too carried away, I want to prepare you.

***

Chapter 1 will be all about the power of thought work, exploring your inner narrative, listening in on your thoughts, how what we say to ourselves day in and day out matters, and staying too wrapped up in negative thoughts matters. So many of us are walking around without ever having given any notice to the soundtrack of our lives, so we're going to spend some time with that album ... is she a chart topper, or does she belong in the trash?

Chapter 2 is juicy and arguably one of my favorite plays on words I've come across in my career. I'm an author right? I love stories, I love hearing them, I love telling them, and I love reminding people to be the author of their own stories. Too often were living out what someone else told us we should, doing it in a way that they said, and believing what they told us without being given the permission to do something different. Well, I am up in here giving out all the permission to *Stop Carrying Other People's Stories and Start Carrying Your Own.*

Have you ever said out loud, "I should be doing ..." finish that sentence however you want. There are a lot of SHOULD be doings that we feel in our lives, again, likely without even knowing it. So, that's what we'll dive into in Chapter 3. Sometimes it's for big things like what career we should have (or should not have) gone into, and sometimes it's for small things like how we should be cleaning our houses or how many throw pillows we SHOULD be having on our beds. The answer to that one is many. But whatever the should might be, it's heavy, and it weighs on you, so we're going to talk about that too.

Chapter 4 is all about the relationship you have with yourself. It is the longest standing relationship you have ever had and that you will ever have, and I don't think nurturing this is talked about often enough. We will explore things like self-trust, self-soothing, self-compassion, and many other things that we'll get to when we get there. I'm going to need some real honesty and vulnerability from you there okay, because you matter.

In Chapter 5, we explore the difference between healthy and unhealthy friendships, and the healing that comes from surrounding yourself with people who uplift and respect you, because that matters so much when it comes to finding joy in your life and breaking free from what you should be doing, or who you should be staying friends with because of time, closeness, proximity ... whatever it might be. Ultimately, I share how choosing myself and letting go of the pressure to chase friendships created space for more authentic, supportive relationships.

Chapter 6 is all about emotions, baby, because we all have them, and we all need to feel them. Like really feel them. In case you were taught otherwise, emotions—no matter how big or uncomfortable—are not weaknesses but natural, human experiences that deserve to be honored. Society conditions us to suppress emotions, especially tears, but suppression leads to shame, anxiety, and even physical symptoms. Every emotion has a place, and we'll uncover how honoring them brings us closer to ourselves.

Chapter 7 is about learning what boundaries are. We will explore why they matter and how setting them can transform your life and relationships. You'll understand why boundaries are essential to self-honoring and that they're bridges that teach others how to love and respect us. Boundaries are an ongoing practice of choosing alignment over obligation, and every time you set one, you deepen self-trust, create stronger relationships, and reclaim your peace.

Chapter 8 is about rediscovering joy, like real, deep, full-body joy. Somewhere along the way, most of us were taught that joy and play are for kids and that grown-ups are supposed to be serious, responsible, and productive all the time. But that couldn't be further from the truth. Joy and play are not extras, they're medicine. They're what help us reconnect with our inner child—that younger version of us who still lives inside, carrying our earliest memories, emotions, and stories.

I share how, during one of the hardest years of my life, I slowly found my way back to joy through the simplest things, and none of it had a purpose or a "result." Whether it's watching a ridiculous reel, singing in your kitchen, or doing something you used to love as a kid, joy is the bridge back to yourself.

Chapter 9 almost wasn't a thing—you'll read about why when you get there. I admit I almost didn't include this topic because it can feel overused or performative like something people say to brush off your struggles. But the more I thought about it, I realized that when practiced genuinely, it can actually save you—slowly, quietly, and deeply.

Chapter 10 is there because most people don't realize this incredibly healing and free resource we have at our fingertips like all the time. Nature is so healing and such a gift, a gift that we're often too busy to remember to enjoy. We are physical, outdoorsy creatures and spending more time outside has so many benefits, so I'm going to make sure that you know every one of them!

***

It's action-packed, this book, and we are going to get to know each other really well. I want to be real with you. I want to be open and vulnerable and share so that you feel safe being vulnerable with yourself, too. Vulnerability is so powerful, but often we shy away from it so we don't appear weak—another story we've been told, that weakness is bad ... I can't help myself, there are just so many! If you are familiar with the personal growth world, then chances are you might also be familiar with Brené Brown's work. If you don't know who Brené Brown is, where have you been living? Just kidding. Maybe.

The basis of Brené's work is around shame and vulnerability. She's spent a huge part of her career exploring these two real and powerful human emotions. Emotions that every single one of us feels, but so many of us hide or run from. We mask it, we push it down, we ignore it, and yet it's the one thing that can connect us all so deeply.

Remember earlier I said we were hard-wired for connection?

Many of us fear others will judge us if we are vulnerable, casting us out and making us feel like we no longer belong, but to be vulnerable and to share is to be courageous. Being courageous is speaking with your heart and leading with love. For real, if you don't know Brené Brown, once you're done here, go give her a search on Google and watch a few of her Ted Talks. (And add her books to the list of must reads.)

If you're not used to being courageous or vulnerable, I want to model that for you so you might feel a bit more open to doing the same. We're about to go on an adventure of breaking free from the shoulds in your life to find more joy and to create more bliss. We're about to explore your stories. All the things that are holding you back will soon be gone.

Are you ready for it? (Fellow Swifties, you feel me?)

CHAPTER 1

The Power of Thought Work

I've already introduced you, like super briefly, to the topic of thought work. In the simplest terms, thought work is really just paying attention to the things you tell yourself and the things that go on inside your head every day. Most of us don't realize the massive amount of thoughts we have in a day and how much they influence our day-to-day experiences and our lives. Did you know that we have at least 6,000 thoughts a day and this can range all the way up to over 50,000?[5] There's also a vast majority of them that are subconscious ones we aren't even aware of, and they ultimately create our reality and they become the soundtrack for our lives—whether it's positive or negative.

Did you know that negative self-talk is a natural and normal part of the human condition?

I didn't until recently, and it was fascinating for me to learn! It also gave me so much relief to know that there wasn't something wrong with me. For so long, I've been operating from the thought process of if I could just get rid of all the negative ways I spoke to myself, then things would be a lot easier for me. It always felt like a constant uphill battle because no matter how much work I spent on listening to my negative thoughts and reframing them, they kept coming back. Or a new dialogue or thought would arise depending on what I was working on or doing and how much I was pushing myself out of what felt comfortable for me. The more I tackled larger things and stepped outside of my comfort zone, the louder the noise became. It was a constant cycle.

It was so reassuring to know that no matter how much exploration I did, those negative thoughts would always be there. If I knew they were always going to be there, then instead of forcing myself to not have them or feeling frustrated when they came back, it instead became about learning to acknowledge when they were there and then making the conscious decision of how I was going to proceed with my life and the situation in spite of them.

Clients often ask me how I got to this place in my mindset, and I have to remind them that it wasn't always like this for me. I like to refer to myself as the driver now when it comes to the thoughts that I have. I am a driver versus a passenger for living alongside and with my thoughts and inner dialogue. This process of getting to where I am now really started with understanding the importance of listening in and paying attention to what those thoughts were. The first step was acknowledgment. When you can acknowledge and question the thoughts, you can start to unlearn, relearn, and reframe the thoughts you might be ready to get rid of, especially the ones that are icky and just aren't fucking true.

Let me break down what this might look like with a recent experience for me.

As I am writing this part of the book it's summer break, which means that my oldest has been home for the last 6 weeks. As a mom who works from home, and also works for herself, (which is such a blessing for our family with having 2 younger kids) this has really thrown off my entrepreneurship, working from home, and being consistently in a productive routine vibe. From September to June, I have an empty house by 9 am and it's quiet until 3:30, which allows for me to have lots of focused time to accomplish the tasks I need to get done in a day. It offers me the predictable routine that I crave to keep me balanced and feeling groovy. During the weeks I balance client work, house work, self-work, and family management.

Summers are a shit show.

Not only have I had 1 child at home with me for the most part since June 30, but there have been many days this summer where daycare has been closed, or my youngest has been sick (all week this week), so that further eliminates my routine, my empty house, and therefore my productivity. There have been lots of thoughts that have come up leading into this summer—and throughout this summer—about that change for me, what that means, and what I could have made it mean about me.

Summer is the worst! I have no time for myself, and no time to really get any work done. Yes, I have thought that multiple times this summer. And in those moments, I had 2 choices, because I noticed the thought, and I didn't like the feeling that the thought gave me. I could stay in that negative spiral and be miserable and grumpy about it, which would have probably made me become resentful or stay frustrated which wouldn't have made me a very fun mom/wife to be around, or I could choose to REFRAME it. Admittedly, old Andrea would have stayed in the spiral and spent her summer bitter and on edge, probably making for a not so fun summer for her kids. Current Andrea—the conversation went a little bit like this, *I know this is not your ideal scenario, but we are just going to roll with it. We are going to make the best out of this time, work when we can, stay present and positive knowing that this is just a season, and that come September we will be able to lean into work and back to a more full income time.* It was such a simple shift in those moments of working on changing the thoughts that have made for a pretty amazing summer so far!

Let me give you another example that I feel like you might be able to resonate with too, because I have been guilty of this MORE times than I would like to admit.

The diet spiral.

Now, I am very anti-diet culture and diet mentality/body shaming etc., but my habits haven't always been that way. I have started and stopped way too many eating plans and work-out regimes, and every time I would stop doing something I started, for whatever reason, I used to really get down on myself about it. Before I did conscious thought work, anytime I would stop something I'd started, I would think things like, *You can never stick to anything,* or *What's the point of starting something else, you're just going to fail,* or *You are such a disappointment.* I would let that bring me down, and it would sit heavy on my mind and spirit for weeks. Not even ONCE taking into account what might be going on in my life at that time that could have impacted my ability to show up. I never considered giving myself grace.

I remember the first time I consciously broke the cycle of that negative thought work. It was February 2019, and I had previously been on a roll with my health, exercising regularly and eating really well—I was seeing a difference in my body. I had been consistently keeping this up for months, when on December 31, 2018, hours before I went to a New Years Eve party, I found out that my had Opa died. And it crushed me. For months.

I was grieving him deeply, and as a result, a lot of things in my life fell to the wayside. Mid-January I got really sick, and it lasted for a few weeks. Coupled with my deep grief, I was not in a great place, but I still remember the compassionate REFRAME I gave myself when I was starting to spiral on the fact that I had missed my workout routine for close to a month. *You've had a really hard past 4 weeks, girlfriend. You need to give yourself some grace here and know that this doesn't mean you're a failure. You are just riding the ebb of life.* There will always be seasons of life that we flow in and out of, and our habits will flow with that, and if we can allow for that to happen instead of giving ourselves a hard time about it, it will be much easier to flow back into those habits when we have the capacity and the space to do so. The pressure was relieved by the power of thought work and reprogramming.

Subconscious reprogramming is such fun work. It might sound silly and certainly doesn't sound super sexy, but it CAN be when you think about all the ways it changes your life and your reality. The ability to change and shift everything you think—literally everything—is what makes it so attractive and exciting to me. It's changed my whole entire life. Not to be dramatic, but like it has.

"**Subconscious reprogramming is such fun work. It might sound silly and certainly doesn't sound super sexy, but it CAN be when you think about all the ways it changes your life and your reality.**"

Let's Get Sciency

Yay neuroplasticity! Have you heard of it?

Neuroplasticity is your brain's built-in ability to *change itself*—to rewire, adapt, and create new pathways (aka ways of operating) based on what you do, think, feel, and focus on![6] It's like the scientific way of explaining what's happening on a biological level when we start to incorporate thought work into our lives. Historically, people believed that our brains were fixed after a certain age, which essentially means once the foundations of thoughts have been laid, there's no way to rearrange, change, or refresh the way we think, act, respond, and behave. Like the roads have been paved and there is no way to tear them up to create new ones, or even fill the holes in the pavement. You know the expression "you can't teach an old dog new tricks," well the evolution of research and science now proves otherwise. Your brain is constantly growing, especially if you are doing intentional work and exploration on yourself, and that means the way you think, react, and even talk to yourself can shift, too. It's like your mind has its own "edit" function just waiting for you to make some upgrades to the roads.

This is especially exciting when it comes to thought work like doing mindset shifts, challenging your inner dialogue, or creating new ways of thinking and living because you're not just *hoping* the changes that you are making are going to stick and become new ways, you are actually TRAINING your brain to think differently, knowing that it will happen. And the more you practice a new story or healthier thought pattern, the more your brain lays down that new neural pathway and the old stuff that's been holding you back fades away. So yeah, it's not just woo or positive coolio ideas, it's legit science. Your brain *wants* to grow with you.

That's not to say it doesn't come without work though, because it does, and sometimes it's hard work, like haaaaaard. Even though our brains are wired for growth and adaptation, they are also wired for safety. To your brain, "sameness" feels safer than "different."

Habits, beliefs, and behaviors—whether they serve us or not—create familiar neural pathways that your brain can travel like well-paved highways. Change, on the other hand, asks your brain to take the bumpy, unmarked back road that sometimes it's never taken before and is worried that there might be a serial killer on so they'd rather not. It's possible, but it takes more energy, awareness, and effort, which is why we often resist it. Cause it's scary!

Part of what makes change so difficult is that we're not just working against our own patterns—we're also carrying the weight of intergenerational influences and societal conditioning, which we are going to explore in the next chapter. The beliefs, stories, and coping mechanisms of those who came before us get passed down, often without question. If your parents or grandparents believed that "this is just the way things are," or they spoke to themselves and operated a certain way in situations, you may unconsciously repeat that narrative, even when it no longer fits your life, or even if it never did in the first place. Change, then, becomes not only a personal act but also a disruption of long-standing family or cultural patterns.

"Part of what makes change so difficult is that we're not just working against our own patterns—we're also carrying the weight of intergenerational influences and societal conditioning."

Stubbornness plays a role too, but not always in the way we think. Sometimes it's not about refusing to change but about clinging to the illusion of control. If I keep doing what I've always done, I at least know what to expect. Trying something new requires trust in the unknown, and that can feel unreachable when we're wired to avoid uncertainty.

The belief that we *can't* change though, that belief alone can be more limiting than any external obstacle. When we tell ourselves, "This is just who I am," or "It's too late for me," we reinforce those neural highways and close off the possibility of building new ones. The brain listens closely to the stories we repeat. If we believe change is impossible, our brain works to prove us right, because it's ALWAYS looking for evidence to support the thought it has, even if it's not true, which is why when we want to change, we actually need to keep giving it evidence of a belief otherwise! And what's beautiful is that when we allow even the smallest opening—the thought that maybe change is possible—we start creating the conditions for the growth that we want. That's where the magic happens.

When you are creating a habit, thought, or behavior change, you are actually out there with a jackhammer breaking away at the old road, the one that's stubborn as hell to rip up, and then you're taking the truck out there to lay some new asphalt. This analogy is probably making anyone who works construction cringe, because I've never actually laid any new roads before, but I am guessing it's like that. It's all a step by step process.

Step 1: Awareness of the thought (which we've started).

Step 2: Repetition, repetition, and more repetition to change the pathway. Please note, this is a real way of breaking it down for you right now. I have been working on myself and consistently challenging the thoughts I have regularly for over 6 years, and I still have to consciously work at it, cause like those roads are hard to dig up.

And if that feels like a bummer, I know, I hear you. I don't say it to discourage you, but I hope it makes you feel a little better knowing that even someone who seemingly "has their shit together" because they launched a book and they coach others still has to work at it almost every day. No one is a superhuman. Whatever profession you're working in or whatever work you have done on yourself, it is still work, and it will always take work. I frequently review the recurring thoughts in my mind, making sure they align with the joyful life I desire instead of the expectations others have placed on me throughout my life. Think of it as regularly weeding the garden that is your mind!

REFLECTION BLOCK

Catch Your Negative Thought in Action

For one full day, write down every negative thought you notice yourself having. At the end of the day, choose one and ask yourself: *Is this true? Whose voice does this sound like—mine, or is it something I've picked up from society or family?*

Thought Work: The first thought I had when I saw the two blue lines on a pregnancy test almost 9 years ago was, I *can't believe I am going to have to undo all the hard work I put in to lose all the weight I lost.* Sigh.

Can you imagine?

A moment that was supposed to be filled with pure excitement was clouded by the fear that I would no longer be celebrated by the world around me for finally being thinner. I always knew I wanted to be a mother (remember the helper and care giver in me) and everything was going according to plan. My husband and I had decided that after we settled into marital bliss for a year, we would start trying to grow our family. We had just gotten back from a trip to the Dominican to celebrate another friend's wedding, and we knew when we got back at the end of October, we wanted to start trying. It was such an exciting time.

We were fortunate enough to not have to try for too long, and on November 20, 2014, our lives changed forever. Side bar: announcing your pregnancy is so weird, it's like creating a post for Instagram, or sitting your parents down to congratulate you for having sex. Random, weird thoughts, I know.

I had dreamt about the day I would pee on a stick, you know, like they do in the movies, and then they sit and wait. The anticipation builds and while waiting, they think about what their baby might look like, what their families will become, and then when that timer goes off, they flip it over and there lies their fate. Yes I have watched a lot of romcoms. Never in my wildest dreams did I think in that moment I would be worried about getting fat again. I was over the moon for what

I didn't know at the time would be our precious Clara, but I couldn't help still feeling fearful of what it would do to my body, and what I would look like post-baby.

That's one story we are sold right. Fitting into the pre-baby jeans (fell into that one), getting your pre-baby body back (yup!), eliminating the mom pouch—all these stories created some real fear for me about what the hell kind of body I was going to be left with after and what I was going to have to do to fix it. Or would it even be fixable? Because all I knew was that after you have a baby, you wouldn't like your body anymore. It's going to be ruined. I was scared by that. I didn't feel ready for that.

I was 26 years old. The pressure to look like I hadn't even had a child consumed me, and I knew something had to change. I was postpartum, and I felt this overwhelming anxiousness about fixing the body I was now living in. It felt so foreign to me and even though it had just done an insanely incredible thing—like you know, grew a human from nothing—I wasn't sure how I felt about it.

I wish I could tell you that was the moment that everything changed for me, but it wasn't yet. From January to June of that year, I remember working out every day with the sight in my mind of me buttoning up those coveted jeans I had from before I conceived Clara. I still remember shopping for those jeans when I "lost all the weight" the first time. I was so proud of myself. The amount of validation I received from the outside about my transformation was hard to ignore, and boy, did I ever get complimented as I wore those size 12 jeans. I had never worn a size 12 before, and I had never been applauded so much by the people around me. As humans, we are hard-wired for belonging, so, naturally, I was amped about being given an acknowledgment of my "hard work." Those jeans symbolized acceptance to me. If I could fit into them again, then I would have known that I made it. Again.

I would try those jeans on about once a week, as a measure of my progress, and the day I was able to button them up and do up the fly, I was elated! I called my partner Mike immediately, in the middle of his workday, to let him know, and I remember feeling disappointed when his energy level and excitement didn't match mine. For the record, my husband is a very relaxed, laid back guy with very chill energy, not really an outspoken energetic human like I am, so I am not sure why I expected such a big reaction out of him, but when I didn't receive it, I was hurt.

When he got home from work that day, I asked him if he would take some photos of me with the jeans on, so that I could post them and share them on my blog and he seemed almost annoyed. "They are just jeans," he said, as he begrudgingly grabbed my phone and took photos. I didn't know why he couldn't just understand how exciting this was for me. I kept posing in slightly different ways, asking him to take more photos, and he eventually just got fed up and told me he was done taking photos.

At the time I didn't realize he didn't get it, because, in his eyes, I was always just Andrea. I was the mother of his child, his best friend, and his wife, beautiful at any size. He didn't see my body for anything other than just a body that he loved and found attractive. He was the one person who never gave me any real validation or acknowledgment when it came to my beloved weight loss (unless solicited of course), because the weight loss didn't matter to him. Although he often told me how much he loved me, and he would always compliment me when I made a point to tell him how my weight loss progress was going, he always followed it up with, "*You've always been beautiful to me.*"

How's Your Life Going?

Huge milestone moments often cause us to reflect on how things are going in our lives. Take the pandemic for example. In March 2020, our lives were globally rocked to our cores. One minute we were going home from school on a Friday before March Break, hearing that schools might not be back in session after 1 week off, and the next thing we knew we were being mandated to stay home from work, not leave our houses unless we were going out for essentials, to stay home and keep away from everyone that we loved. The parameters of the lock downs and the shutdowns varied from country to country, heck they even varied from province to province, but as measures were lifting, coming back down, and then lifting again, many of us were reflecting on the things that were working for us and the things that were no longer serving us in our lives anymore.

I still can't even believe we went through a time like that as a population. The fear, the uncertainty, the choices we were forced to make, the choices that were made for us—the trauma, the violence, the division, the awakening … we went through this entire thing collectively, and now most people barely talk about the fact that it even happened. It's like it was all a bad dream, one that we woke up from, but are impacted more deeply by than a lot of us realize.

Some people chose to not return back to the jobs they had previously done for the last decade.

Some people were re-evaluating the people they spent their time with.

Some people were reflecting on how they filled their calendars all the time, and when they were suddenly, unwillingly cleared, they were thinking about what they actually wanted to fill their calendars up with again. We made decisions about which family members we were willing to break the rules to see and which ones we were happy to use the pandemic rules to not have to see for a while. We did the same for friends too. Some friendships survived and some didn't make it. We reflected on which memberships and monthly subscriptions we were happy to let go of to save money, and which ones we couldn't wait to be able to use again.

Many of us evaluated how we had been taking care of ourselves up until that point too. I know I did. At that time, there was still a lot of fear and unknown as it related to the virus and many of us wanted to make sure we were taking care of ourselves better so we didn't find ourselves sick and needing to access a healthcare system that was already overrun with sickness. (What a fucking time to be alive can I just say that was.)

And as a result of all these reflections on our everyday habits and routines, as well as our lives overall, though some of us stayed status quo, others made some pretty significant shifts. Quitting the job, ending the relationship/friendship, saving money, and nourishing our bodies more with food and movement. Ultimately, some really great things happened for some of us for both our mental and physical health. I know I, for one, have not been the same since then.

We might do this type of total re-evaluation of life when we experience a loss too, especially if it's someone who is close to us and if that loss is sudden. We do this when we get married, or when we become parents perhaps, but without a big event or milestone, we don't often take a step back and do a little inventory to see if we are really *happy*. We don't take a step back to see how many things we are doing for other people and how many things we are actually taking the time to do for ourselves. The funny thing, though, is that whether we decide to consciously do that reflection or not, our soul knows and our heart knows. As much as we ignore it, or don't pay any attention to it, our bodies and minds are hardwired to experience bliss and joy—it's something they crave when those feelings aren't present. What do you think happens when we aren't experiencing these things on a regular basis? I can share with you something that I know for sure, and it goes a little like this.

You have been mothering and working your full-time job for the last 10 years, and it kind of feels like you have been in the trenches for a while, but you're holding out for *someday*. You have an incredibly full schedule of extra curricular activities for both kids, which take up 4 of your evenings during the week. On those evenings, once you leave the office and get home to grab the kids, it's a rush for dinner, either before or after the activity, and then after the activity it's homework, bedtime routine, and then bed. Once the kids are in bed, there are a few things that rotate on your roster: catch up on or fulfill any other work things that need to get done, you catch up on housework and laundry and dishes, you binge your show and shut your brain off with your favorite snack, or you crash and go to bed early because you can barely keep your eyes open. On the nights the kids don't have activities, you try to get to a fitness class, or the gym or go out for dinner with friends, *maybe*. And on the weekends, you're still catching up, you're spending time with your partner, but not a lot of time with yourself and with your own thoughts... maybe because they aren't the nicest and you try to avoid them at all costs.

Living like this for a while catches up with you, though. It's likely that your body might be holding onto the elevated levels of cortisol, tons of unaddressed stress, no downtime, the lack of self-care and prioritization of yourself, the running everywhere all the time, and you are starting to feel unhappy. Since you've been conditioned to think that if you're feeling unhappy, you might need to lose weight, it leads you to stepping on the scale, and then based on the number you see you decide that you do, in fact, need to lose weight.

So, you embark on a journey of restriction and misery and guilt. You may have even done this before, but you think that it's going to be the thing that brings your joy back, and it's going to work this time. You start the first week off really strong in your mind. You were able to get up in the mornings and workout, even though you were exhausted. You were able to say no to dessert all week, and to your favorite muffins at the office, and you feel proud. You were down 2 pounds at the end of the week, and you finally felt happy and accomplished. The second week came around, and it felt a little bit harder. Things got more demanding with your schedule, the weeknights were busy, which meant you went to bed late a few nights, and then you missed 2 morning workouts because you were too tired to get out of bed. You know how this goes right? At the end of the week you are still the same weight, you haven't lost anything, and you feel hopeless. The cycle continues. And you're still not happy.

This is the solution we have been conditioned to explore for as long as I can remember: you aren't happy, so you get skinnier because that helps. The diet industry is really fucking big AND it only profits if people continue to believe that it's going to be the thing that solves all their problems and that it will make them happier. Women need to be distracted with diets and the way they look so they don't try to find joy in other ways, like using their voices and speaking up for themselves and basically taking over the world. We're onto them.

Going on a diet and exercising specifically to lose weight doesn't make you happy my friend. Happiness, like real beautiful happiness, comes from doing things that light your heart up. It comes from movement to show your body love, it comes from doing more of the things that you love for yourself, taking time for yourself, setting boundaries, speaking kindly to yourself—all things that the diet industry can't sell you. All things that come from within.

This would be the time where I tell you it's helpful to take some time to REALLY inventory your life. *Ugh, I know, right!* To take a step back, as though you had a huge milestone, a life-changing moment, and reflect on how you're spending your time, on what is making you happy, and on what you no longer need to hold onto, what is no longer serving you, and what can you release.

Totally get it—it *sounds* like a lot, but doing a life inventory doesn't have to mean disappearing into the woods for a week or going on a big retreat (unless you want to, which I also recommend). It can start with something as simple as getting quiet with yourself and your favorite super cute journal—no phone, no to-do list—and asking yourself a few honest questions:

What's feeling good right now?

What's draining me?

Where am I just going through the motions?

You can journal it, or you can even voice note it, or talk it out with a trusted friend. The key for something like this is just realness and honesty. You gotta be real with yourself, and furthering that, give yourself permission to let go of the stuff that's not aligned anymore, even if it once was. Think of it like de-cluttering your life's emotional closet. **What are you choosing to keep, and what are you ready to release?**

For years, even decades, you've been led to believe if you're unhappy and unfulfilled then there is work to be done on the exterior. This is typically connected to weight loss, and they tell you that when you lose the weight, then you will be happier. Ta dah!

"We're all trying to be happy and at home in our bodies in a world that sells us all the reasons why we shouldn't be."

We're all trying to be happy and at home in our bodies in a world that sells us all the reasons why we shouldn't be. Things and reasons we have been sold and told by the world around us that create the perfect storm for us to constantly seek on the outside to find our true happiness. This cycle and this constant searching for more is something we learn from a young age, and if we aren't careful, it can stay with us until the time we leave this earth.

But I am here to remind you that there's more to life. There is more to life than diets and self-hatred as a solution to our lack of fulfillment. There is more than pushing yourself at the gym 7 days a week to get the life that you want. There is more than weight loss and restricting what you eat. There is more to living miserable, in a toxic relationship with others, and with yourself. There is more.

Okay, I got side tracked again. Back to the pre-baby jeans and the post-baby weight loss.

It took me some time, but I slowly started to learn that things could be different, and if I was going to be a role model for my daughter, then things really needed to be different for me. It had to be about more. It had to be about more than just fitting back into the jeans I wore before she was conceived. There had to be more than just trying to get skinny, to make it look like I hadn't even had a child. So. Messed. Up. Have kids, but don't look like you have, *ew*. This is when the real inner work started for me.

Little by little, I expanded the conversations I was having with myself and with others. Little by little, with my daughter watching and as my motivation, I learned more about true happiness. I healed. I read books and sought out all the personal growth that I could. I was eating it all up, and I couldn't get enough. I mean I wrote a book about it, for crying out loud!

It felt like I was back in college again, reading *The Four Agreements*, because I started to really explore the impacts of all the wounds from my childhood and adolescence (wounds that we all have, just in varying degrees of difference). I started gaining more of an understanding of how they were impacting and dictating the person I showed up as in my life and in my relationships. I started to entertain the idea that maybe I didn't have to try so hard to change the body I was living in, instead that I could look at it with kindness and honor for what it had done for me, which for the record is a lot! We don't give our bodies ANYWHERE near the amount of credit they deserve. Like it shows up for you every day, right? You wake up, you get out of bed, you breathe, you walk, you run, you laugh, you enjoy life. It does that for you. Every damn day. That is love—love is showing up for yourself every day, but I wasn't giving my body love. Not in the slightest.

So, I started to explore loving it, accepting it for what it was in that moment and in that season. I learned and developed the knowing that transformation and happiness could go beyond the scale, and in fact they most certainly did. I realized and started to live out true healing.

Healing and transformation aren't in what I thought about my physical body, but instead it stemmed from how I chose to think about myself and the world around me every day; the conversations I chose to be a part of, and the things I chose to consume, both in physical and psychological nourishment.

Turning inwards and taking care of your soul, while also taking care of your body, is the path to bliss.

Oh and shit-talking yourself just doesn't fly down this path either.

I often think about the number of years I wasted in some of these mindsets, how many awful things I've said to myself, and things I have done to myself out of hate and spite, but not for too long, because if I do that, I get pissed at all the time wasted I could have been pouring into other things. But as many of us do, I fell victim to the stories, and they got me from a very young age.

When I talk about the "stories" I mean the scripts that go on inside our heads, which are created to help us navigate this world. It's composed of all the input coming at us regularly as well as all the input we've received, and that shapes who to be, how to act, and what to believe. It's also known as our inner narrative. These are the thoughts that pop into your head throughout the day, what you believe at your core, what your morals are, and what your internal dialogue is. We're about to go into that thought work talk again.

For each of us, this inner dialogue (our thoughts or stories), have come to us in many different forms. They come through our childhood experiences and exposures, which is often tied to our family dynamics and family core beliefs because your family is the first agent that you are influenced by. They teach us all that we know, both good and bad. Then, as we grow up and go out into the world, we start to be exposed to other sources of information like the education system, mass media, social media, and peers. And all of a sudden we are taking on so many things at rapid speeds we barely have time to process them before they solidify themselves in our brains as neural pathways and as a result, become our inner narratives or stories. All this happens in our formative years too, which means we are soooo susceptible and so impressionable without the ability or the wherewithal to be curious about whether the conditioning and the stories are true or helpful—or not.

As I became a young adult, I really felt the pressure of the stories. As I shared with you earlier, I carry a lot of internal dialogue about the size of my body; I also carry a lot of inner dialogue about how people perceive me, care about me, and value me, and this has impacted my confidence for decades.

Let's be real, our minds are kind of wild. They're constantly chattering away, creating stories, jumping to conclusions, and spinning out worst-case scenarios. Thought work is about learning to slow that mental chatter down and start questioning what we're actually thinking instead of just believing every random thought that pops into our heads.

As we have already discussed, we tend to accept our thoughts as facts—they sound like truths, but really, they're just thoughts. And not all of our thoughts are helpful, not all of them are true.

Thought work is like shining a flashlight into a dark room. It helps us see what's really going on in our minds instead of stumbling around bumping into things and wondering why we feel stuck or off. When you become aware of your thoughts, you get to decide what stays and what gets kicked to the curb. That's powerful.

It takes a ton of practice and awareness. You won't be perfect at it. I'm definitely not. But over time, it helps you feel more in control, more grounded, and more aligned with the person you actually want to be.

And this work has truly changed everything for me.

CHAPTER 2

Stop Carrying Their Stories and Start Living Yours

I have been actively doing thought work for the last 7 years.

Thought work: actively observing, managing, and monitoring what the heck is going on in your head (in case you missed that earlier). Remember when I told you how many thoughts we have in a day AND that many of them are subconscious? Yeah, there's a lot going on up there all the time.

Prior to those 7 years, though, there wasn't a lot of INTENTIONALLY thoughtful focus going into the thoughts and the stories going on in my head. I wasn't paying any attention to the soundtrack on repeat in the back of my mind. Instead, I was just moving through life, not fully understanding how much the stories I had heard and was carrying were affecting me, the way I felt about myself, and how I was showing up in the world. This is one of those, *the more you know the better you can do*, and also the *we were doing the best we could with what we had at the time* scenarios.

I remember when my maternity leave with Clara was ending; it felt daunting. I was not ready to go back to work. There was something about the conventional 9 to 5 lifestyle that no longer appealed to me like it once had. I couldn't quite put my finger on what it was about the structure and rigidity that I didn't want anymore. Of course, looking back, I can now see that was the start of my heart whispers. My heart and soul were yearning for more—I didn't know how important it would be, but the desire to create my life and my schedule was rising within me.

I knew all too well that I would soon be back to the routine of corporate life. And if you've done it before or you are in it right now, you might know it goes a little bit like this: get up in the morning, get my daughter up, rush to get her to daycare so that I can get to work for 9, work all day until 4:30, leave work, do kid pick-up, get home to do dinner and then bedtime routine, all while trying to spend some quality time with her, keep up with the house chores and maintenance, spend time with my spouse, and also have time for myself so I don't go crazy. 5 days a week, rinse and repeat. I cringe just thinking about that lifestyle for myself—it does NOT feel like the right life for me. Over the years, I have learned the importance of leaning into the things that feel right for you, and maybe that structure of time away from the house DOES feel good to you, especially if you are in a different season than me. That's okay if it does. We are allowed to have our OWN opinions and still share the same air if we do, that's the beauty of being humans, our differences.

As my return to work date got closer and closer, and when I thought about the transition, all I felt in every inch of my body was nerves and anxious energy. I felt anxious, partly because

I wasn't ready to be away from my daughter so much, and partly because I worried about finishing everything I needed to. Being away from that type of hustle culture for the last year had truly been amazing and a break that I didn't realize I needed. I really enjoyed our slow mornings, something I had really come to appreciate. Slow mornings meant cuddling in bed, coffee in comfy clothes at home, and a leisurely breakfast together filled with laughter. We would play together, we would take walks, we would do anything we wanted to, we would spend time together, just us. We had our routines. I would cook lunches and dinners, and that meant dinner was on the table when Mike got home from work (not something he expected, but something I really enjoyed being able to do for him). I could do laundry during the day, tidy the house during nap times, and work on my coaching certification so that when she was in bed at night, I would unwind with Mike and we could just watch a show or talk and catch up after the day. I would also have time for myself to decompress and just exist doing the things I loved and that lit me up. I had a strong feeling that when I went back to the corporate work structure, it would not look like that, and I really feared how rushed our life would feel.

Turns out, I expected just right. Funny how that happens.

My return to work created rushed mornings and difficult circumstances on the mornings when my daughter didn't want me to leave her, or when I was caught up in traffic, or late getting out the door because I was trying to figure out the timing while rationalizing with a 1-year-old who was on no one's schedule but her own. This routine and life left me with crippling anxiety almost daily within the first 6 months. My nervous system was going through a total shock, while really also still being in postpartum.

Did you know that it can take up to 2 to 3 years for a woman to fully recover from childbirth, both physically and mentally? Facts. And I am certain that was playing a part in it for me.

I was still nursing her—I nursed up until 19 months so I imagine there were some feelings of separation I was going through too. It wasn't just the difficulty of the new routine, it was my soul longing for something different and me not feeling like it was accessible any other way, partially because at the time, I didn't really know what that difference I was searching for was. Running errands after work was difficult; my mind raced with to-do lists. My longing for Clara was so intense because I already felt like the days were so short that the tightness in my chest prevented me from leaving my car sometimes. There was this one day I needed to return something at the mall on my way home. I remember pulling into the parking lot, and I physically could not get out of my car, I felt paralyzed with this feeling that I just needed to be with her. I sat there for a little while in the car in my parking spot, in tears, just trying to muster up the courage to get out of my car. After a while, I decided I couldn't do it. I turned the car back around and drove right to her daycare, picked her up, and brought her home. When we walked through the door, I sat down on the front bench in our house at the time. I picked her up, put her on my lap, hugged her, and just cried. I tried to take deep breaths snuggling her into me, just to help calm me down. I don't think I've ever told anyone that before. I felt like such a bad mom at that moment, needing to hold onto my child to help calm myself down.

"I picked her up, put her on my lap, hugged her, and just cried. I tried to take deep breaths snuggling her into me, just to help calm me down. I don't think I've ever told anyone that before. I felt like such a bad mom at that moment, needing to hold onto my child to help calm myself down."

I experienced bouts of severe anxiety sitting at my desk at work, just thinking about what I needed to get done at home that night, and I often wondered what Clara was doing all day. I remember one day in particular at work; I had an afternoon meeting with the leadership team and as the time for this meeting approached where I had to do reporting on where my work was at, the anxiety in my chest was building. Instead of thinking about the meeting, all I could think about was wanting to escape, to run. I was in full fight or flight.

In an attempt to try to bring myself down, I went to the back part of our office building where the finance department and some empty offices were. I went into one of the offices, shut the door, turned off the light, and sat on the floor behind the desk, trying to breathe. As I was having more and more of these episodes, I was understanding the course of them in my body. They would come on with a feeling of butterflies in my chest. After a few minutes, that feeling of butterflies would escalate into full-blown panic. My heart would race, my vision would become tunneled, and most times I felt like I couldn't take a full, deep breath. This would be the peak. After the peak, some deep breaths, sitting with my eyes closed, distracting myself, talking with someone, things would slowly de-escalate, the whole episode usually lasting about 15 minutes. It was exhausting, it was debilitating, and I knew I couldn't go on like that. I had never considered myself to be someone who desired to be a stay-at-home mom, but on days like that especially, I wished more and more that I didn't have to be tied to a 9 to 5 source of income to support my family.

Until this point, I didn't know that entrepreneurship was a thing. I didn't know that people could make money while being at home and by not working for someone else, but I was slowly being introduced to the idea in small ways, like glimmers of hope. During my maternity leave, I uncovered my passion for helping women achieve healthy lifestyles and wellness routines, so I enrolled in a 12-month certification online to become certified as a Holistic Health Coach. Being a part of this program introduced me to alumni, colleagues, and other humans who had taken the same education and had started working in business for themselves. It was a whole new world for me, and I glimpsed the potential of a life my soul yearned for. That's what I wanted and didn't know. I wanted to work for myself. I wanted the freedom to be at home, to make my schedule, but also to make a living. (For the record, I am writing this chapter on a Friday afternoon and this is what my day has looked like so far: dropped Clara off at school, did swimming class with the baby, put baby for a nap, did some client work, had a consultation and now I am here writing—I am literally living out my dream of time freedom—fucking cool!)

After learning about this whole other world of possibility, I looked into what entrepreneurship might look like for me. I didn't know anyone else who worked in a service-based business for themselves. Mike had his own carpentry business, but I had never considered something like that might be possible for me in the same way.

I spent months researching the prospect of being a coach and running my own business. I thought about developing hourly coaching rates and designing programs. Group coaching was something I understood more, so I dreamed up the real possibility of what life could look like. I mapped out what it would mean for me and for finding my bliss in life, because let me tell you, I was not feeling much bliss in those days.

That year, in 2018, I made the leap and registered my coaching business. It was actually a lot of fun coming up with a name for my business because I had never done it before. I spent lots of time thinking about what I would want to do for people and how I would want them to feel when working with me. I wanted a name that would symbolize change and transformation. What would people be searching for when they reached out to me and hired me as a coach? That's when it became clear. When I looked for that certification I spoke about earlier, I knew I wanted to explore a career that supported people with way more than just what they ate. Although what you eat and how you move your body is important, it's not everything. I knew that the balance of life existed for people when they focused not only on what they ate and how they moved their bodies, but that the way we loved ourselves, the way we felt about ourselves, and the way we spoke to ourselves had a ton of value too! When all of these things were focused on, they would be the things that created balance in our lives. In turn, we would feel more happiness, more peace, and more joy ... we would feel more bliss—and that's where the name of my business came from.

Balance + Bliss

My business has since evolved over the years, as I have learned and grown more, but the foundation has always been there. It's always been about finding balance and bliss in your world and uniquely what that means to you. I think the most important piece to it all is that it has to be you, for you, and feel good for you. Over the years I have been told that people struggle with the word balance because they wonder how it's possible to balance everything in their lives. I usually follow up their question by saying "It's impossible." Certain things at certain times will require more of your attention, but if you can keep YOURSELF balanced (pouring into all the areas that support you), then you'll feel more calm, supported, collected, and well going into the never ending juggle of life.

When I finally came up with the name and registered my business, I was so excited to share with people in my life who were close to me, including my mom.

I vividly remember having a conversation with her where I was sharing about what I had been working on over the last couple of months and what my dreams were for pursuing coaching full-time. My plan was to leave my full-time *9 to 5* job as soon as I could to coach and to have more of the time freedom to do what I was understanding was really important to me. Her response was something to this effect: *Why would you leave your job, with benefits [and security] to pursue this dream? You have a family to think of now and this is a risky move. I don't think it's a good idea.*

Let's unpack this a bit, because those of you who are thinking, Wow, that's a rude thing to say, might want to understand where this could come from. First off, I can assure you there was no ill intention when she said that out loud to me. She loved(s) me and only wanted what was best for me, and is often my space to bounce things off of. The reason I am sharing this story with you is to provide some perspective and maybe give grace to the people in our lives who don't know any better and also to show the depth of the stories we carry in our society and how they play a part in everything we do, say and believe.

What you are seeing here is a carrying of stories playing out in real time.

Let's break that down a little bit.

We are deeply and heavily conditioned by society and the world around us from the moment we are born. Most of us don't really realize how much it drives us (until we do of course!). Society conveys expectations to us both directly through instruction and teaching, and indirectly through what we observe and witness. Our beliefs, our behaviors, our life goals, milestones, relationships, aspirations, roles, rules, and abilities are all a product of societal conditioning.

In school we learn academic subjects, because as we get older, we want to be smart so we can apply to school, to the career we want (which we must know right away at 18 when we are applying), and then we can graduate and move into that career. When we choose that career, we are told that the best option is to choose a job that pays well, that has good "job security" so we can provide for our families.

Societal conditioning also indirectly tells us which jobs are more favorable and come with higher standings through the media and television shows that we consume. *Has somebody ever told you they are a doctor, dentist, lawyer, pilot, etc., and as a result you have made some sort of instant judgment based on that? Has somebody ever told you they are a cashier, bartender, server, buser, in the food service industry, driver, customer service etc., and as a result, you have made some sort of instant judgment based on that?* (No shade to you if you have or if you are in any of the listed industries above, it's just another demonstration of how deep our programming and stories run.)

Long before we EVER realize it, we are carrying other people's stories, narratives, and beliefs, and, worse, we are believing them like they are our own.

Like my mom and her belief that security and smarts only come from working 9 to 5 for someone else and that entrepreneurship is too risky if you have a family.

Because this conversation happened prior to all my true thought work, I can't even begin to tell you how discouraged I felt after that phone call. I found myself second-guessing and questioning everything I had spent the previous 6 months working on. Everything my heart and soul were telling me about my longing for more and my desire to help others in this way felt foolish, risky, and naive. At that moment, I immediately started to take on her story without even realizing it.

Fast forward to now, CLEARLY I didn't let that story stop me (I was always one to push back against what I was being told to do, sorry mom), but I would be lying to you if I said it didn't grab onto me. It certainly did slow my progress to getting to where I wanted to be. By picking up someone else's story and carrying it as my own, I made a lot of hesitations and scared moves in my pursuit of coaching and speaking instead of bold ones.

As I grew my coaching business, I began branching out into local women's groups to connect with others and share what I was building. I also joined virtual entrepreneurial communities, knowing I needed to put myself in new and different spaces if I wanted to attract clients, build relationships and connections, and to make my business work.

I knew I wanted to work with clients 1:1, but I was also open to the idea of supporting groups of women. Still, in the beginning, it felt incredibly uncomfortable. Growing up, we're often told not to talk too much about ourselves—that it might come across as boastful or "too much." Add in the taboo of talking about money or selling, and suddenly, I was in totally unfamiliar territory.

Sharing what I did, inviting people to work with me, even standing up in a room to talk about my business—it all felt awkward and unnatural. And the inner stories running through my head didn't help: *Who's going to want to work with you?* or *You sound strange asking people to hire you.*

My business wouldn't have made it very far if I had let those fears and limiting stories keep me quiet. My profession is built upon sharing your own personal stories, challenges, and victories so you can show other people what's possible for them. I NEEDED to talk about myself. Like this book, WTF would I have even written about then. Lol

What are the chances that you are carrying stories that were given to you by other people or ones that you picked up along the way and believed as truth?

"Sharing what I did, inviting people to work with me, even standing up in a room to talk about my business—it all felt awkward and unnatural."

I had been working with a 1:1 client for a short time when she shared with me that one of the things she wanted in her business was to make more money. Although this was a goal she had, there was something that kept getting in the way of it. She wasn't talking about her offers, and she wasn't charging enough for them in order to have the big financial success she was hoping for. As part of our work together, we were developing and fine tuning a new direction she wanted to go in her business, but there were some stories she was carrying which were getting in the way. I knew it, and I was excited to help her realize it too. There was some mind trash that needed tossing to the curb.

When the topic of charging more for things came up, it seemed like something she was uncomfortable talking about. She even made the comment that she doesn't need to be super rich, she just wants enough to be comfortable. I was curious about that. *What is wrong with being super rich?* I asked her. I went on to share that if she were super rich, it might allow for her to give back to her community and invest in her business in ways she wouldn't be able to otherwise. What I slowly started realizing was that she had a *story* about what it meant to be rich … a *story* about what type of person that meant you would be if you were rich. As we continued our session, I just flat out asked her, "What is it about being labelled as, or seen as rich that you have an aversion to," because I could feel it in her. I had a hunch that she had a perception about what it meant to be rich, and I wanted to know more. See, that's what we do as coaches.

"Coaches aren't people you hire to do all the things for you and give you the answers to what you want to accomplish—instead they are there to help you find and uncover the answers within you."

Coaches aren't people you hire to do all the things for you and give you the answers to what you want to accomplish—instead they are there to help you find and uncover the answers within you. Most times they are already there, but societal conditioning, the people in your life, and the stories you have and believe block you from really being able to find the answers. I love that part of my work.

Speaking of answers, the answer I got from my client was exactly what I was expecting. We uncovered that growing up she knew people who were wealthy and had seen that being wealthy and having lots of money meant you didn't care about other people. Around her, the people who were rich were selfish, greedy, rude, unkind, and only worried about themselves. She didn't connect the fact that she too could be rich, because she didn't see herself as someone like that. She was kind, thoughtful, and committed to helping others. The story of being rich and being a jerk was playing loud in her head, and in order to embody that rich energy and identity, we needed to re-write the story.

Once I learned this about her, part of our work became re-writing the story in her mind of what it meant to be wealthy, to find examples of people who were rich, kind, and caring, and by doing this, she was becoming open to the possibilities of seeing herself as someone who could be rich too! We started to change the story she was carrying about abundance and created a new one she could carry that was her own.

Is it possible that there are places in your life where you are carrying stories that aren't your own?

REFLECTION BLOCK

Past Patterns, Present Choice

Think of a belief or script you grew up hearing (about your body, work, money, relationships, etc.). Write it out. Then write the new belief you want to create for yourself, one that aligns with who you are now.

I titled this chapter **"Stop Carrying Their Stories and Start Living Yours"** because I already know the answer to that question is yes, and I want you to really consider what you are carrying. What do you believe about how you should look, who you should be, what you should be doing, how you should be living, what you should be asking for, or where you should be that isn't serving you one bit. What are you carrying that's literally stopping you from doing the thing, being the person, asking for the thing you want to do and be?

Are you not asking for the promotion because one time when you were 7 Aunt Jeannie told you that you were too bossy and you took that as a bad thing? And now, even though you love the idea of being a leader, you're worried that people are going to look at you differently?

Are you not allowing yourself to be in a loving relationship because some dick head told you in a fit of rage one time that you were unlovable, and now you indeed believe that you are unlovable?

Are you being a martyr of a mother, running yourself completely into the ground, forsaking your basic needs, your desire for rest and joy, because society has made you believe in order to be considered a good mother, you need to be completely selfless, not daring wanting to do something for yourself? And now you're resentful, but you also feel bad for being resentful.

Maybe these things resonate with you—maybe they don't. Maybe your stories aren't as loud or as identifiable, but I am going to take this moment to strongly suggest you take some time to figure that out. *Pausing for you to go, where the hell do I start?*

Don't worry, I got you.

Awareness is the first step to re-writing the stories or simply just letting them go.

For as long as I can remember, I have carried the story that people didn't really like me. They didn't like me, they found me to be annoying, that they only tolerated me to my face, but that at any moment those people around me, those who I thought were friends, would just leave me, abandon me.

This is a script and a narrative that has been playing in my head for as long as I can remember, and it's the one I've had to work the hardest on pushing back against.

When I was in high school, I became quick friends with this girl, and before I knew it we were completely inseparable. We were together every day after school and had sleepovers almost every weekend, on the weekends I was not with my dad. We told each other everything, and it felt like we could always rely on each other. You can likely all remember having a friend like that.

"For as long as I can remember, I have carried the story that people didn't really like me. They didn't like me, they found me to be annoying, that they only tolerated me to my face, but that at any moment those people around me, those who I thought were friends, would just leave me, abandon me."

At some point though, a shift happened in our friendship. We still spent all this time together outside of school, but when we were at school, she started to ignore me and treat me differently. In our shared groups of friends, she would laugh with, talk with, and sit with everyone else but me. She gave me the cold shoulder, and as you can imagine, I was so hurt and shocked. I didn't understand what was happening, I didn't know what had changed, and whenever I tried to confront her about it, she dismissed that anything was different, told me to stop worrying about it, and even said to stop asking her about it.

One particular weekend, we were having a sleepover at her house, and I was made pretty aware that she had received an invitation to hang out with someone else but that she had turned it down because we already had plans. We watched a movie like we did most Friday nights, and she spent most of that time on the family room computer messaging with them. When the movie was done, she told me she was getting picked up shortly and that I should stay at her house and wait for her, because she would be back in a couple of hours. So that's what I did. I sat there, at her house, for HOURS with her parents there, waiting for her to come back. I spiraled deeper and deeper into my thoughts of not being good enough for her to want to spend time with me, to stay with me, and wondering what I could have done differently to make her want to stay, to value time with me.

I will share more about this in a later chapter and how it has shown up in my life, but as you can imagine that shit hurt deep. It was a foundational moment in my formative years that I will never forget—and that I definitely created some stories about.

These stories show up in our lives, time and time again in new friendships we form and new relationships we have because they are a part of it. And like I was saying earlier, they will continue to stay a part of us and keep us stuck in a cycle of the way we're living until we decide to put it down. To unpack it and to decide it's no longer ours. It's no longer a part of who we are and the person that we want to be.

And is this a quick fix, no.

And does this take time, yes.

And is it hard work, also yes.

The stories that we've been carrying for decades don't heal overnight. Awareness may be the first piece of that puzzle, but it's important to remember that unlearning takes patience, it takes grace and it takes commitment. Almost every time we have a goal to get healthier, to lose weight, to want to be happier, we look around at the things we can fix quickly, the things that are going to get us the fastest results, with the easy road to get there.

And then, time and time again, we find ourselves in the same place, feeling the same way. I think it's because we have got it all wrong. While moving our bodies and how we fuel ourselves is so important, the absolute most important thing is what's going on in our heads and what's going on in our hearts. The stories we've been given will stay with us until the day we die if we never make steps to change them.

Like me, completely blowing things up to create this reality that I have now. There's no longer room in my head, my heart, and my life for things that don't serve me well.

7 years after we had our first daughter, we became pregnant with our second daughter Eloise, and because of all the decisions past me made, as well as all the thought work I was doing, I was excited for a do-over when it came to creating my reality within my own terms.

Flexible mat leave, being home for my Clara when she needed it, sending Eloise to daycare 4 days a week instead of 5 so I could just be home with her one of the days. Being able to do laundry in the middle of the day, work during any hour I want to, all because I made a conscious decision to only carry my own stories, to live unapologetically in a way that makes sense for me and for our family. And gosh does that feel so much lighter.

What we're carrying, saying to ourselves, believing about ourselves, and living out that's not ours can be the heaviest thing of all.

So let's start learning some new stories together shall we?

CHAPTER 3

The Shoulds are Heavy as Sh*t

I was sitting in my therapist's office for our second session when I had a revelation. I had just spent the last 20 minutes trying terribly to fight back tears unsuccessfully while I shared with her how I had been feeling. The ache and the anxiety were fighting to get out, I could feel it in my chest, the tightening. The anxiety and the message it was sending was tired of being ignored, and I was exhausted.

I had recently started up therapy again after a long hiatus. The last time I saw a therapist was when Clara was around 2 years old. I was back to working full-time hours after my maternity leave, as I mentioned earlier, and I was having a really rough go. I knew that I needed to get some support before things got even worse. I started seeing this incredible human who was helping me to work through my crippling anxiety. At the time, she gave me some invaluable tools to help me see the reality of my life, my thoughts, and my situation, and it helped me to move forward and leave the anxiousness behind. To this day I still use some of the tools she gave me.

Almost 6 years later, I was seeing someone again, because I had just gone through a significant episode of burnout. Let me give you some context.

At that stage of my life, I was parenting a 1-year-old and an 8-year-old. I had finally quit my secure, stable job, after working toward the goal of leaving since my maternity leave ended in 2016 after having Clara (remember the story I told you earlier about the dream life I knew I wanted to create. It took that long). I was completely and utterly exhausted from spinning my wheels and moving non stop. I love entrepreneurship, but it is not for the faint of heart, and at times, it requires a ton of time, energy, and resources. After I had Eloise, although I was on a leave from my part-time teaching job, I was certainly not on leave from my coaching business, and in true Andrea fashion, I saw maternity leave as a period of time where I would be off not as the chance to rest and recover and be with my last baby, but as the chance for me to really lean into my business and have it grow SO much that I didn't have to go back to a "corporate job." It felt like my opportunity to finally do it. And I jumped right in.

I took a short break that included renovating our entire en-suite because the shower door fell off when I was showering the day we came home from the hospital—man is that a story!

When Eloise was born in the middle of 2022, we were STILL living through some covid restrictions in certain medical settings, including our local hospital. The rules on the maternity ward were that visitors would be very limited and that no children were allowed on the floor, except for the ones being born, of course. I felt awful that not only would I have to leave my older child to go and give birth, but that we would be away from her for the 2-day c-section recovery period, and she wouldn't be allowed to come and visit us, let alone meet her new baby sister. It was really hard to accept that she wouldn't be able to visit. I was that woman calling the floor, trying to negotiate for my 7-year-old—who was not disruptive and would be super quiet—to be given special privileges to come and see her sister after she was born, very politely of course. Unfortunately, it was not going to happen, so even though adults could come visit, which I still to this day don't understand, we didn't allow any visitors at all. It wasn't okay to me that others would have the chance to meet her first. This is relevant to the story I promise.

My c-section was scheduled for the morning of July 29th, and by the time I got into surgery, Eloise was born healthy and gorgeous at 12:15pm. It's pretty common for new parents to feel very unsure with this new little human and for them to want to take full advantage of their chance to stay in the hospital for 48 hours to get the most help from the nurses. Being a new parent is a wild time when you feel like you have no clue what you are doing, and you are still getting to know this little human.

Nurses on the floor joked that we were veterans. This wasn't our first rodeo, and they knew we were eager to be discharged so we could take little sis home to meet the older one. They told us that I needed to stay for 30 hours, but if I could show them I could walk, if I went #1 and #2, and the baby was eating and passed her tests, then we could be discharged early. I had a goal. I don't think I was ever more determined in my life as I was to push through the excruciating lower abdomen pain to stand up and get to the bathroom so that I could pee into the little measuring cup. Numerous times Mike and the nurse told me I could take a break and try again later, but I didn't want to—I had another baby to get home to.

In the short time we were there, once the drugs were out of my system—cause that took some time post surgery—we hung out and continued binge-watching *Chicago Fire*, which was our show at the time. I nursed, we watched, I ate, we bathed the baby, and we only spent 1 night at the hospital, because at the 36th hour post-surgery, I walked out of that hospital and went home to my child. I would be lying if I said I wasn't in pain though. The first thing I wanted to do when we got settled at home was take a shower. I was encouraged to lay down and rest, but I just wanted to get showered so I could really rest. I gave the baby to my mom, who was dying to snuggle her, and turned the water on. I couldn't wait to stand under the running water to feel like a clean human again. Between the surgery, NBD, passing out from the IV and sweating profusely, the recovery, and the diapers I was wearing, it felt like I hadn't showered in days.

And now we're at the whole reason I started this story.

Not long after I was in the shower, I heard a strange noise right before the GLASS door literally came off the hinge—like it just broke, and the door started falling toward the ground. Like a mothers instinctive reflex, I turned and grabbed the door before it smashed to the ground, luckily. We then had to shower with no door, with a towel clipped up to catch the water for a couple days before we started the renos to put in a new shower. Eloise's first outing was to the bath depot to look at shower stalls when she was DAYS old. New moms are super heroes.

So like the first 6 weeks of her life weren't exactly relaxing.

Back to the book, so for the first 6 weeks after I gave birth I tried to heal from surgery and settle into life with 2 children, but then I went back full force into business. Full disclosure, I didn't even really shut down during those 6 weeks, as my business was often on my mind, and I would work from my phone while being still during feeds and snuggles.

When I geared back up, I was also running my podcast—a fully self-produced show I might add—that was launching new episodes every week. I was working the business, running the podcast, managing and leading my third co-author project, considering starting another new business, writing this book, planning for a 100-person massive event that I was running with 3 other women, running a household, healing from child birth, trying to re-establish a regular movement and workout routine, navigating being a mother of 2, trying to have time for myself, not to mention being a wife and partner … the list goes on.

For real. Like I said, burnt out.

Managing all of that, especially during the summer with 2 kids at home, juggling day trips, nap times, kid time, and work time was exhaustively fulfilling. It's so strange how something I looked so forward to also felt so heavy at times. I felt like I *should* be enjoying it, it's what I wanted. And I *was* enjoying it, but I was also so ready for the summer to end so I would have routine again, because quite frankly it was a lot.

That September when Clara went back to school, I started to ease into the routine I was craving … or so I thought. In retrospect, when I think back to that time, I think my body and mind had made it to the proverbial finish line and now that they were there, they were shouting, *enough is enough!*

I had been feeling off since the start of school, a little more anxious than usual, and like the tasks that were on my to-do list, tasks I *should* be excited to do, were feeling extremely heavy. One night, I sat down with Mike to watch a movie, and I knew something was off. I was staring at the TV—from the outside it probably looked like I was watching it—but I wasn't watching it at all. I was actually unable to absorb any of the content in the movie. I felt dazed. The only way I can describe what was happening to me was I felt like I was having an out of body experience, like I was floating above myself, completely unable to connect with what was happening. As I sat there snuggled under a blanket on the couch, staring at the TV, my mind was somewhere else, everywhere else.

I can't even pay attention to this movie.

What is going on with me?

Why can't I focus?

*I **should** really edit that podcast episode.*

A million other thoughts and the sensation in my body that something wasn't right.

I was putting my head on the pillow at night, feeling like a bear was chasing me in the woods instead of feeling ready to fall asleep. I was so tired, but I couldn't relax. I would lay there in the dark feeling like my heart was beating out of my chest, my mind racing. I felt fearful and panicked about what was happening to me. I had never experienced this before. Looking back, I know now that my nervous system was in overdrive.

"The only way I can describe what was happening to me was I felt like I was having an out of body experience, like I was floating above myself, completely unable to connect with what was happening."

That month, I got sick with hand, foot, and mouth disease after Eloise brought it home from daycare. I lived for 5 days with sores on my hands and in the back of my throat. It was one of the most painful things I had experienced. I then came down with an awful sinus cold. My head was so heavy, I could barely focus. As a result, for another week, I lived with one ear constantly plugged. My face was breaking out in a rash, first a scab on my nose that wouldn't heal and then hives around my eyes. My body was screaming at me, both inside and out. And I still hadn't even considered that my plate was fucking overflowing.

All of this happened in the span of two weeks. And I am as certain as you are reading this you can probably see how my body was sounding the alarms.

Maybe something like this has happened to you too.

In the middle of that month, I was away on an overnight with 2 dear friends that I actually almost canceled because I was feeling so unwell. I cried as I packed my suitcase the night before leaving, and I cried to them in voice notes saying I didn't know what was happening to me. I told them there was no sense in me coming because I wasn't at my best and that I wouldn't be much company, and even though they gave me the option to stay home, they encouraged me to come and talk out with them what was going on with me. So I went. We stayed in the room in our robes, laid in bed and watched a show, ordered pizza, and I pretty much cried the whole time. So much crying, my body was losing control, and I felt like I was losing it too.

It's worth noting here that these 2 friends are also incredible life and business coaches, and this situation is the perfect example of why having the right people in your life and in your corner can really turn things around for you.

In true coach fashion, and in the most gentle ways, they asked me all the right questions that got me thinking about just how much was on my plate, like how much was *really* on my plate. They encouraged me to reflect on how much time I was spending in all of the places, how thin I was stretching myself. They helped me to realize there were things I needed to delete before I pushed myself over the edge, an edge that I was already so close to.

In real time, we workshopped how much time each project was taking me, discussed my goals for the future of my business and my life, and had honest conversations about the mental capacity all these things took up, and, most importantly, what it was doing to me. Exactly 1 month from that day, I was set to deliver a keynote speech at an event and I feared that if I continued in the same way, I would be in no place to show up for that event. For something that meant so much to me.

You see, even if you are passionate about many things like I am, all those passion-driven things still take up space. They take up brain space and calendar space and energy space, and contrary to what I was thinking and how I had been operating for 14 months, I am not a superhuman with endless amounts of energy (WHAT!). What I was doing was not sustainable, nor was it good for me and my mental health. I needed to make a decision.

"I thought that if you love what you do, you will never work a day in your life. That's what society has sold us, that's what I believed. In truth, I was drowning."

I needed to let things go.

But I felt like I should be able to do it all. I thought that if you love what you do, you will never work a day in your life. That's what society has sold us, that's what I believed. In truth, I was drowning. I was drowning in my passions and in my life. I was not truly taking care of myself, not at all.

I felt like a fraud—I *should* be better at this.

I *should* be able to self-produce my own show, because I know how to do it.

I *should* be able to move my body regularly, because I know it's good for me.

I *should* be able to work this coaching business and all the things that means, because I love it and it's what I wanted.

I should.

The shoulds can feel really heavy, my therapist said as I sat across from her in that second session together. Profound.

The shoulds are heavy as shit, I thought.

REFLECTION BLOCK
The Weight of "Shoulds"

Make a list of the biggest "shoulds" you're carrying right now (e.g., things you tell yourself you *should* be doing as a parent, partner, entrepreneur, friend, or just as a person). For each one, ask yourself: *Where did this "should" come from? Is it really mine, or did I pick it up from someone else's expectations?*

Before my epic cry, I had just finished talking with her about the way I was returning to taking care of myself. We celebrated the ways in which I had been keeping my calendar a little more empty than I had previously that year. We discussed how I had been feeling a lot more leveled since the deletion of the things. (Therapy is a roller coaster eh?)

One of the things I had set as a goal with her for the last session was to continue focusing on the plan of staying out of burnout, sticking with the current things I had kept on my plate, and to not take on any more. The one thing I had been still struggling with was fueling my body well, making the decisions that I know make me feel better, and taking the time to prepare wholesome meals. Oh, and movement.

I should know better, I told her. I knew the things that made me feel great, and yet I still struggled to implement them.

She asked me if the term *self-pressure* resonated with me. I immediately laughed. That was a full body yes. She asked me what the laugh was for, and I told her it was incredibly on point.

I was putting so much pressure on myself for the things I know that I SHOULD be doing, and it was creating so much self-pressure that my internal dialogue was literally blocking me from leading with love.

I was putting so much pressure on myself from the stories I was carrying about what my capacity *should* be, what I *should* be doing, how I *should* be operating, that I was completely ignoring my intuition, the signs my body was giving me, and how important I know taking care of myself is.

There are a lot of things in life we feel like we should be doing. I know you feel it too, because no one is immune.

You're a business owner—you should be hustling.

You have a family—well, you should be visiting them regularly, even if it's toxic.

You have kids—well, you should want to be spending all your time with them.

You're a wife—well, you should put your husband's needs first.

You're an employee—well, you should be available to your employer at all times.

We all walk around bearing the weight of these shoulds, some of them harder to carry than others. Remember those stories we talked about earlier, those play a role here too. Beyond that, beyond the stories from other people, there are so many stories and shoulds we place on ourselves.

What are the things you think about on the regular about what you should be doing?

How much is thinking about those shoulds preventing you from having more joy, having more ease, and having more peace?

The shoulds are incredibly heavy to carry. By starting to set the shoulds down—one conversation at a time—you slowly allow yourself to move instead into a place of flow, only leaning into and doing the things you truly want to do, the things that light you up, and the things that bring you joy.

I had a conversation with a client once about keeping her house clean. Like me, she really appreciated a clean and tidy space. It was something that made her feel peace and calm week after week, but sometimes she found it hard to get the cleaning done because she dreaded doing it, calling it a mundane task. We talked about how she cleaned and what she did to keep her entertained or motivated while she was tidying up. Did she listen to a podcast? Watch a movie in the background? Dance it out while listening to her favorite playlist? She shared with me that she did none of those things. She cleaned in silence, in quiet, and focused only on the cleaning task. After more conversation, it turned out that when she was younger, her mother told her *how* she *should* be doing her cleaning. Cleaning was a serious task, and because of that, it was not meant to be fun. You *should* be focusing on what you're doing and be doing it with no distractions. SAYS WHO?! (You can likely imagine how the rest of that conversation went between us, haha!)

I told her cleaning can be done in whatever way feels good for her, that she was free to explore doing it, in HER OWN home, the way she wanted to, not the way she was told she *should* be doing it. She didn't realize how that story she had been carrying from her mom about how cleaning should be done had been impacting how she enjoyed her life and the things in it now.

REFLECTION BLOCK
Doing It Your Way

Identify one area of your life where you're still operating under someone else's rules or expectations.

Ask yourself: *If I gave myself full permission to do this in a way that feels good for me, what would that look like? How could* making this shift bring more ease or freedom?

Together, at that moment, we made a pact. She was going to clean while she listened to music or watched TV, and she was going to make it FUN because that felt good for her. She decided she wasn't going to do it the way someone else said she should, she was going to do it her own way.

She did it her own way, and that small revelation made such a difference for her.

I will ask you again, what are you doing in your life in a way that someone else told you you *should* be doing it, and how can you do it for yourself instead?

CHAPTER 4

Your Relationship with Yourself, Above All Else

I remember when I hated the reflection, I saw in the mirror. I hated it so much that I avoided it at all costs.

I can't tell you how many hours I've wasted over the years thinking negative thoughts about myself, negative thoughts about what I was capable of achieving, of what my body looks like and how people around me perceived it. Change it, shrink it, hurt it, hate it. (*Did you just read that to the tune of Busta Rhymes's song Touch It? If you didn't, are you singing it now?*)

I still remember that rock bottom moment just after college like it was yesterday. I shared a little bit about this moment in my first book, and it was a time when I hadn't stepped on the scale in a while. After seeing a photo of myself at our college graduation party, I had been spiraling so deep into my negative thoughts, I couldn't stop them, and I needed to see how much I weighed. I couldn't stop thinking about how unhappy I was with the way I looked and how angry I was at myself for looking that way. Gosh, how poorly I spoke to myself in those moments. It was late at night after everyone else at home had gone to bed, and I was having trouble getting to sleep. As I lay there in the dark, by the glow of my alarm clock, watching the minutes go by, I couldn't stop the thoughts from racing about that photo.

Maybe it was just a bad angle.

I definitely wasn't ready for that photo, maybe that's why I looked like that.

This is why you don't take photos anymore Andrea, because this is what you look like in them.

It doesn't matter how hard you worked to graduate college, you can't keep any of these photos for memories, you look horrible.

I vividly remember when my earth shattered because the scale said 255. I was devastated, and the thoughts I had, the things I was saying to myself, only got worse. Sometimes I wish I could go back to that moment in bed and give my past self a big hug. I would sit with her while she cried, wipe away her tears, and tell that younger version of me the number on the scale has nothing to do with how lovable, kind, and worthy she was, or how successful she would be in changing other people's lives one day. She really could have used some love in that moment, but I also know that girl going through those moments, doing what she did with it all along her journey, are what made me the woman writing these pages for you right now. I'm so proud of her. It's part of me reconciling with all the versions of myself and acknowledging that they brought me to these days of my life. Like the butterfly effect—imagine where I would be if she hadn't walked the path I walked since then.

The number on the scale that night and the self-hatred I felt was the catalyst for the next 3 years of what I like to call my first transformation (the second one came when I worked on the things that really mattered after my daughter was born, the things I am sharing with you in this book that you're reading right now). I never allowed myself to miss a workout, and if I did, the way I spoke to myself about missing that was complete trash. I restricted myself so much when it came to the things and the foods that I enjoyed, and I only praised myself when I could stick exactly to what I was supposed to be eating. I spent those years chasing an external body ideal, completely missing the mark on all the internal healing that needed to happen in order to fully embody what living a blissful life meant. I guess I just hoped that by fixing the outside, it would subsequently fix my shitty internal dialogue. There was a complete absence of understanding the importance, and quite frankly the necessity, of developing, prioritizing, and nurturing any kind of relationship with myself. But you don't know what you don't know, maybe like you right now, or it's just something you forgot about, and we are giving grace to that version of me and extending it to this version of you too.

Speaking of giving grace, this period for me wasn't a complete write off because I flexed that dedication and motivation skill in a way I never had before. I accomplished a big goal that, in a way, I had never had before, and that was a big deal. I learned a lot during that time, and while I got the success I was looking for, I often reflect and realize that not once in the journey to what I thought was health had I ever considered how I spoke to myself or the relationship I had with myself, and, when it came down to it, how I treated myself day in and day out.

You teach people how to treat you by the way you treat yourself, you know. It's as simple as that. People will love you fully in the same way that you love yourself. And yet, most of us spend our entire lives doing for everyone else, and showing up for everyone else, while continuously treating ourselves like an afterthought. Have you ever taken a moment to really consider the fact that the relationship with yourself is the longest relationship you're ever going to have? Take a moment for that thought right now. **The relationship you have with yourself is the LONGEST (and most important) relationship you will ever have in your life.** Longer than any friendship, any partnership, any fleeting situationship you'd rather forget. You are literally stuck with yourself for life. Or blessed, depending on how you look at it.

I never remember being taught to love and care for myself the way I was taught to for others. As kids, we're taught to be kind, to share, to help—but all of this is only about how to interact with OTHERS ... What about us, yo? I was never told to turn that around on myself. No one sat me down and said, "Hey, you should also be kind to yourself. Check in with yourself. Celebrate yourself the way you celebrate your best friend. Be nice to your body and kind to your mind." But like, these things are so crucial to your health, wellness, and happiness. If you consistently speak to yourself negatively, it really affects you. There's no time for it!

Fun fact about me: if you are in my company and you say something negative about yourself, you might just hear me respond with, "HEY—don't talk about my friend like that!"

We grow up measuring our worth through the lens of other people's approval.

"You teach people how to treat you by the way you treat yourself, you know. It's as simple as that. People will love you fully in the same way that you love yourself."

Think about it: How often do you wait for someone else to validate you before you allow yourself to feel good about something? "I'm so proud of you!" hits differently than "I'm so proud of myself." It's like we feel the need for someone else's stamp of approval before we can believe we're doing okay. Can you imagine if you did things the other way? It feels weird in the beginning, though I'll be honest with you. It feels silly. And it feels selfish. It feels vain. It's unfamiliar. Own that ... for now. But hear me out ... What if, instead of seeking validation externally, we started asking ourselves, *Am I proud of me?* And if you dare to answer it by saying yes, celebrate that, and let that be enough. WOO!

REFLECTION BLOCK

Internal vs External Validation

Reflect on a recent accomplishment (big or small). Did you wait for someone else to notice or validate it before you allowed yourself to celebrate? How would it feel if your own acknowledgment and pride were enough? Write about how you can begin shifting from external to internal validation in your daily life.

Fancy psychologists call this external vs internal validation. Studies show people who rely too heavily on external validation struggle with self-esteem and resilience.[7] When our sense of self-worth depends on what others think, we're constantly at the mercy of them, moving in our lives to make other people happy, to please them, or impress them, which creates this identity of abandoning yourself. On the flip side, when we focus on developing a strong internal validation where we acknowledge our own efforts and achievements, give ourselves our own pat on the back—this leads to higher confidence, better emotional regulation, and overall life satisfaction.[8] Things we all want and need but aren't always quite able to name.

Yes, it might sound like a tall order, and you might wonder how the heck you would ever get there. Like I said earlier, these things don't happen fast or overnight, but they can happen. Try not to expect anything fast to happen overnight so that you don't set yourself up to fail. Instead, we can start by slowly shifting that response, that feeling of discomfort and that current vanity story.

You can start by trying this, for example: The next time you accomplish something—big or small—take a pause and acknowledge it. For real!

Got through a tough day without losing your cool? That's a win.

Finally started that book you've been meaning to write? (Or finally wrote a chapter after having let the manuscript sit forever … me right now … but also, YAY ME!)

Met a deadline at work?

Crushed a good workout?

Took an unkind thought and swapped it into a new one? Celebrate it.

Start showing up for and speaking to yourself the way you would for a friend. If your best friend told you she finally started therapy after months of debating it while she was going through a tough time, you wouldn't just nod and move on. You'd tell her how proud you are. (YAAAAASSS girl, bring on ALLLL the healing!) Why not do the same for yourself?

When you treat yourself with the same level of care and respect you so graciously give to others—sometimes even the ones who don't deserve it—your mind will start to shift the way you view yourself. Over time, this becomes normal operations for you, and THEN comes the cool part ... people take notice. Even if it's subconsciously, they notice and then they adjust. They'll either rise to meet the energy that you're putting out, or they fade out of your life (especially if you're no longer takin' their shit)—and honestly, either option is a win. When you set the tone for how you want to be treated, you naturally attract people who align with that standard, and then, life starts to become really cool.

Take a moment and think about the people in your life.

Do they respect your boundaries (we're going to talk way more about boundaries in another chapter)? Do they uplift and support you? If the answer is no to either of these questions, it might be worth examining whether that's just how they are or whether you are unintentionally setting that precedent for yourself. People learn how to treat us by the way they see us treating ourselves. Let me give you an example. If you are constantly overextending yourself for others, saying yes when you are exhausted, tired, or should be saying no, and never carve out time for yourself, you're signaling to the world that your needs come second and that they aren't valuable enough to come first. If you brush off compliments or downplay your achievements, you're showing others it's okay to do the same or that you don't feel worthy to receive them.

"When you treat yourself with the same level of care and respect you so graciously give to others—sometimes even the ones who don't deserve it—your mind will start to shift the way you view yourself."

Think about this as you're reading:

How are you treating yourself?

Are you showing up for yourself the way you show up for your people?

Are you speaking to yourself with the same kindness you give to a friend?

Are you acknowledging your wins, your growth, your effort?

No? Maybe it's time to start. The way you treat yourself... that's the blueprint. That's the standard. That's what we show others and can expect from others. It's what teaches the world how to treat you in return.

And it has to come from within, it just has to.

REFLECTION BLOCK
Blueprint for How to Treat YOU

Make a list of the ways you currently show kindness or encouragement to your closest friend. Do you show up this way for yourself? Where is there a gap? How can you begin closing it so the way you treat yourself matches?

I had a revelation in 2024 in the office with my therapist (you're getting the therapy trend here).

This was another therapist that I was working with; she was a couples therapist, and before we dove into joint sessions together, she had a session with each me and my husband to learn a little more about us, which I thought was a really cool part of the process. She learned about what made us tick, how we were raised, and got a better understanding of our child-hood experiences, because these things show up as patterns in our relationships. They always show up because they are so connected and they run the show if we don't realize it.

Since having taken what I did in college and all the exploration I did, I knew that what we experience as a child as we are learning our way in the world, and the things that we go through in our family home, have a direct impact on how we show up in relationships. I have loved learning more about that, given how committed I've been to growing and the relationship I have with myself. Plus, like you will learn in a later chapter, we really needed this if we were going to move forward in a way that felt good for both of us.

But our therapist dropped a revelation to me I had never considered before.

I've always known I didn't like conflict. When people hurt me, I rarely shared that with them. I didn't ask for what I needed, and I hated when I knew people were upset with me. Historically when it came to conflict, I had always been the first one to smooth things over, sometimes to a fault. I hated sitting in the discomfort of conflict, and, more importantly, I sought out validation from the person I was in conflict with to make me feel worthy again and to help regulate the anxious feelings I was having.

If you know anything about our nervous system, it operates on a bit of a cycle. There are two main cycles or systems, if you will, the sympathetic and the parasympathetic nervous system. When we're under stress, the sympathetic nervous system (SNS) takes the lead—it's like our body's built-in "fight or flight" mode. It's what makes your heart race, your breathing speed up, and your muscles tense. Basically, your body's getting ready to either face the challenge head-on or escape from it. So, if you're in a heated argument or just feeling the pressure of the moment, your body is reacting by getting you into that fight-or-flight state.[9]

Once the stressors are gone, the parasympathetic nervous system (PNS) steps in to help us calm down. It's like the body's natural "chill out" button, helping things return to normal so we can rest and digest.[10] Either we get this return to balance from external factors or, like we teach babies, we soothe ourselves.

In these types of situations in the past, whenever I needed the stress feeling to be gone, I looked to someone else to do it. And this was me all the time in conflict and arguments that came up in our marriage. I hated the tension (result of my childhood), and I didn't like to live in it for very long. I always looked to my husband to solve arguments with me right away so I could bring down my nerves to be validated and brought back to homeostasis. My partner and I have different conflict management styles. For him, when there is tension, he needs to retreat, sit with it, process it, and then come back when he's feeling more calm. I am the opposite, so time and time again, I was never getting that ability to regulate with him.

Because of this, I often reached out to friends when we were having a fight. They would talk me down, listen to what I had to say, and that helped me to get calm, to bring my system down, and return to baseline.

"The more I thought about it, the more I realized I had never really learned to adequately self-regulate. 36-years-old and I'd never really intentionally leaned into doing this for myself."

I was telling my therapist about this pattern of how I had lived my life and how this pattern existed in our relationship, and she asked me a simple question: *How do you self-regulate?* She was curious to know how I took care of myself during these moments of upset, or unrest … How was I supporting myself, strengthening that relationship with myself? The more I thought about it, the more I realized I had never really learned to adequately self-regulate. 36-years-old and I'd never really intentionally leaned into doing this for myself.

At the root of this … I hadn't built enough trust that I COULD regulate myself, instead I was looking at others all the time to support me. Now don't get me wrong, there is nothing wrong with leaning on the people around you for support, guidance, and love, but you also have to be able to rely on yourself. If everything and everyone in this world around you went away, you would be left with you and yourself. And if you haven't spent the time to foster and grow that, you are doing the relationship with yourself such a disservice.

It's been a new thing I've been learning since then. This next lesson in being a student of myself and learning what helps me to self-regulate during these times has been kind of fun exploring. As I've developed the tools that help me during these moments, they've become tools that also then help me in other moments of my life. In many of life's moments, I keep learning I can confidently lean on myself and tell myself that everything is going to be okay. Instead of my default being to turn to a friend, or to force my partner before he's ready, I've worked on building the trust within me to rely on myself to return to that parasympathetic state. And let me tell you, this has been particularly freeing for me.

Let's stay on this topic of self-trust for a minute, because I have found this to be a real game changer for the way I interact with, believe in, and communicate with myself, which of course ultimately feeds and fuels the relationship we have.

Have you ever heard of the term self-trust? During a 2024 group coaching program I led, I was amazed to find that many people lacked understanding or knowledge of self-trust. No joke when I tell you that self-trust is often at the root of anything new you want to try, and most positive and healthy conversations you are having with yourself involve an element of this. (Yes, I talk to myself often, and you should too—don't worry, by the end of this book I hope you will be!)

Experts define self-trust as firm reliance on your own integrity. It centers on a powerful belief in one's own abilities, integrity, and judgment. It's a belief in yourself and your decisions, even when facing challenges or setbacks. It's not just about believing you can do things, but it's also about trusting your gut instincts and making choices that align with your values.[11]

Self-trust forms the baseline for how you experience your life. When you trust yourself, you have the courage to follow your own internal compass. Which is so powerful and freeing. You're more likely to be true to yourself, which can lead to deeper and more authentic, meaningful connections with the people who choose to let into your circle.

When you trust yourself, you treat yourself more like a friend. You're less likely to engage in mind trash dialogue, hurtful stories, or other people's stories because you're always looking out for yourself, which can lead to greater emotional well-being.

Self-trust is like the foundation of safety and security that is built within yourself, and the stronger it is, the less you will look to others on the outside. Key components of self-trust include: self-compassion, honesty, acting in your own best interest, being comfortable to challenge your own limits, believing in love, the absence of judgment, and radical acceptance, to name a few. It's a really special place to live within yourself.

When you have self-trust, you always have someone on your side or in your corner and, beautifully, that someone is you. *Insert smiley face and little giggle here because I was beaming ear to ear writing that line.*

A time that comes to mind for me when I took what felt like the biggest leap in trusting myself was when I joined an adult glee group called Pop Nation for the sole purpose of leaning into fun and joy and healing again. It was the most rewarding experience, but it didn't come without hundreds of moments where I could have spiraled into major self-doubt.

What you also need to know, though, is that I did not grow up dancing, or singing, other than alone in my house, of course. I had never been on stage or part of a performance before, but I still felt drawn to do it. In order to get into the group, you had to submit an audition, which basically involved me singing a song to the camera and sending it off to be watched by the organizer (a micro moment of self-trust). I was excited when I received the email confirming my acceptance into the group, but was equally nervous about what that meant. It meant I was going to have to ACTUALLY get on stage to do the thing.

I really enjoyed our first vocal night. I can't quite describe the feeling of being in a room with over 100 other adults and not only singing but harmonizing together. Full body chills. I left that night feeling hopeful about my decision to join the group. The first choreography night, however, was a very different inner experience.

The structure of the group was that we got together once a week. And each time we met, it was a back and forth between learning the full tune/harmonies and road map of the song on vocal nights and learning the full routine for a song on choreography nights. That first dance night felt like a disaster. There was only 1 night to get through the complete song, so the instructors couldn't spend too much time on each move or section of the song to ensure that everyone got it. Instead, they taught you a part, went over the steps a few times, both with and without music, and then they moved on to the next part. Literally just as fast as it took you to read this section.

I was a mess. I couldn't get the moves, and the more I couldn't get the moves, I was in my head about not being able to get the moves. "Dancing is just like walking with style," the choreographer told us, and I thought to myself, *you a damn crazy man*. I kept going left when we were supposed to go right, and I kept pointing down when we were supposed to be pointing up, and like how the fuck was I supposed to make that arm circle while also swinging my foot around and posing? I tuned into my inner dialogue really quickly that night:

You had NO business signing up for this. You are not a dancer, and you have never danced this way in your life.

You have no rhythm. Choreographed dancing is NOT like dancing at the club.

Is it too late to get my money back?

I am going to be the only one on that stage who does not know what they are doing. I am going to look stupid, and I am going to ruin this whole routine for everyone.

I spiralled. Just then, the guy beside me asked me how I was doing. Maybe he saw the look on my face. I told him I was really struggling with the moves, and I was kind of getting in my head about it. And right there, he reminded me about self-trust. Not quite in those words, but he shared with me he'd been dancing for many terms, and the next sentence he said became the record in my brain for the next 5 months as I built myself up to get onstage. *It always comes together on show weekend.*

I believed him, and then I remembered to believe in myself.

I spent the rest of the class shifting the inner self-talk to something different. I built security in myself by exercising the self-trust I am always continuing to develop. I told myself that I WOULD get it. I told myself I had a ton of time to practice, and that in 5 months, I would get it. I set myself up for the belief, *What if come show weekend, you surprised yourself?*

I allowed self-trust to seep into every part of my brain that day, and for the weeks that followed—and by show weekend—you bet your bottom I was on that stage, moving through every routine like the back of my hand. I gave myself the space to move through my perceived limitations, to challenge them in a way that felt safe, and to show myself what was possible for me. And that my friends is how you build a deep sense of self-trust, in the micro moments.

What do you believe about what's possible for you?

This element of deep self-trust isn't something I built over night, and it's also not something that is innate within us, either. Depending on what you've experienced growing up, what traumas you have been through, and how people have treated you in the past, it's likely that your self-trust has either dwindled over time, or maybe it wasn't even something that was nurtured into existence in the first place. If you've lived through violence, your self-trust may have eroded as frustration built for letting yourself be in that situation (likely unconsciously). If you grew up in a home where no one listened to you, or where others always decided things for you and you never got a chance to think for yourself, you never developed that skill.

Think about how trust is built in the friendships and relationships you have or that you are starting; usually it's built by that person showing up for you when you need them, both when you ask them to, and especially when you don't. You build trust through kindness from them and when they show you they care. Trust is built through safety and comfort. It's built when you say something negative about yourself, and that person shows up with 5 compliments about you and tells you not to speak about yourself that way. **HYPE.**

"I had to learn that no amount of weight lost, no milestone hit, no praise from others could ever replace the work I needed to do on the inside"

You build trust with yourself the SAAAMEE way, my friend. A deep knowing that YOU will always be there for YOU. That you will always treat yourself with kindness and care. That you will always provide yourself with safety and comfort. (This is making me emotional as I write this.) That YOU get into the habit of interrupting that negative thought and that YOU replace it with 5 compliments. The love that you are looking for has always been you and that sets the tone for how everyone else treats you.

REFLECTION BLOCK

Self-Trust Check-In Prompt

Think about the last time you doubted yourself. Did you calm yourself down, or did you turn to someone else right away? What could you try next time to trust yourself more and feel steady on your own?

The way I treat myself sets the tone for everything else in my life. Literally everything. I used to think self-love was just about liking what I saw in the mirror or reaching a certain goal, which is why that rock bottom moment felt so hard for me. I didn't know it was so much deeper than that. It's in self-trust, it's in the way I speak to myself, the boundaries I set, the way I validate my own experiences instead of waiting for someone else to do it. It's giving myself a big fucking hug when I need it. I spent so many years chasing external approval, believing that if I just looked a certain way or achieved a certain thing, I'd finally feel good enough.

I had to learn that no amount of weight lost, no milestone hit, no praise from others could ever replace the work I needed to do on the inside, which is why at 50 pounds lost, my first thought when I got pregnant was about gaining weight again instead of being able to sit in the joy that I had just created life! Learning to show up for myself, to be my own biggest cheerleader instead of my worst critic, has been a fundamental change. And let me tell you, once you treat yourself with the same kindness and respect you give to others, E.V.E.R.Y.T.H.I.N.G shifts. The people in your life adjust (or kindly see themselves out if you're lucky), your confidence grows, and suddenly, you're not waiting for permission to feel good about yourself—you just do.

Realizing how much I relied on external validation to regulate my emotions, especially in conflict, made all the difference. I was putting my peace in someone else's hands. Learning to self-regulate, to sit with my feelings instead of immediately seeking reassurance, has been uncomfortable as heck but also necessary. And honestly, it's strengthened me in a way that I never knew was possible. Now, instead of panicking when things feel off, I remind myself that I am my own safe place, and I don't think I would have really learned this tool without the support and kind encouragement from our counselor. Outside support is always worth it.

And speaking of worth, my worth isn't dependent on someone else, and neither is yours, boo. The way we treat ourselves will always set the standard for how the world treats us in return.

CHAPTER 5

You Deserve to Be Treated Like You Matter— Your Relationships with Others

At the end of 2022, I was recording an episode for my show, *The Balance and Bliss Podcast*, and the episode was a reflective one. With the plan of starting 2023 off on the right foot, in advance of recording, I had spent some time thinking. I considered what I wanted to let go of and leave behind in 2022 that was no longer serving me. Then I thought about the direction I wanted to go with my life and the healing I was continuing to do. I like to think of it kind of like cleaning out your closet. This process is always a good idea because it prevents clutter from building up—it gets the things that you are no longer wearing out, and it allows you to organize things that need to stay so that when you walk into your closet in the morning all that's there are the things you love to wear. When you are wearing things that make you feel great, then it means that you can naturally show up more badass in your everyday life. It's just science, lol. This practice was becoming a more regular part of my routine because it was becoming incredibly important for me to live more intentionally, and I wanted to share it with my audience in an episode to encourage them to do the same (kinda like I am going to be doing for you too, right here, right now!).

During things like the full and new moons, or at pivotal times like the turn of the new year, it's helpful to think about what's going on in my mind, my life, and my relationships. Like I mentioned earlier, our thoughts are plentiful. A regular inventory, or "eavesdropping" on what is going on inside your head, in your heart, and in your life can help to make sure that things are always serving your highest good, or happiness and bliss.

Once the inventory is done, I take some time to review what feels good and what doesn't. What feels good stays, and what doesn't feel good doesn't. The end. I just let that shit go. Letting it go can look different depending on when I am doing it. If this practice is part of a full moon ritual, then I might write the thoughts or feelings down on pieces of paper and burn them as part of the process, whereas other times I might journal about them, or I may just take a mental note and move differently in the future.

For the podcast episode, I shared a few thoughts on what I had decided I was going to let go of at the end of that year. Kind of like a public declaration. One of the biggest things I had decided I was letting go was chasing people and forcing friendships. This one really had a hold on the little girl who never wanted to feel left out or forgotten, or that she was not included. At 35-years-old, though, I knew I was still carrying so much baggage from friendships I had been a part of in the past and that my need to be liked was still taking up way more brain space and worry than it needed to.

For as long as I can remember, I have always wanted people to like me. And while I think that this is a pretty common feeling for most people—especially women—I felt like my desire was unhealthy and to my own detriment most times. We want to be liked, we want to feel like we're a part of something, and we want to feel connected to other people. This has been deeply true for me, but to a fault, and it was still really affecting me.

Because I lacked confidence and craved acceptance, I allowed people to treat me poorly for years. I have often felt like I was on the outside of the group, always trying to fit in and be chosen, wishing I was the main one people called on. Yes, I am an over-thinker. Yes, I have the tendency to worry about everything that I have said for hours and days after it happened.

REFLECTION BLOCK

Choosing yourself

What does "choosing yourself" look like in your friendships right now? How would your relationships shift if you believed you didn't have to chase love, approval, or inclusion?

Let me tell you a story.

I was on a mastermind call with a bunch of other women who are in business for themselves. We met once a week to check in, celebrate wins, brainstorm challenges, and give each other suggestions or creative ideas. During this call, one woman was talking about how she was currently in the process of launching an event and unfortunately it was not receiving the type of interest she had been hoping for. I could connect with how that felt, both as a fellow coach and as a human. It can be really hard to put yourself out there, time and time again with no interest, and I wanted to offer her something to help her through the thoughts and feelings that come with that (the helper in me). After she finished sharing, I offered her the advice that had once helped me improve my approach and achieve better results.

When I was done talking and done sharing, she had a ton of follow up questions about my advice; other people chimed in and shared their thoughts about what she could do as well (ideas that I quickly convinced myself were better than mine) and she said she was feeling much better and appreciated the chat. Once we hopped off the call, I spent the next hour thinking about the advice I had given and the PERCEPTION I had about how she received it and what she really thought about it. I started to convince myself she thought I had given her poor advice and that everyone else in the meeting also agreed with that thought because their advice was different from mine. That thought led to me being worried I shouldn't have said anything at all and that they wouldn't want me there in the future because of the "stupid" thing I said.

It was eating away at me so much I even reached out to a friend I have in the group and told her what I was spinning about. This friend is someone who I had really connected with and someone who is such a supportive and non-judgemental sounding board. She is one of the many people I have in my life right now who are helping to heal the old friendship wounds I have. She was talking me through it and at the same time I decided I needed to also message that person who was looking for advice, to check in with her.

I sent her a voice note on Instagram saying I was just checking in about the advice I had given and I hoped it landed okay, that she felt like it was helpful, and basically I was wanting to make sure it hadn't upset her (I was worried she wouldn't like me anymore). Remember when I said the PERCEPTION I had about what happened—well here's what actually happened. She was so glad I had checked in. She said she had planned on sending me a message as well to thank me for my advice to let me know that it was great advice! It had encouraged her to ask more questions about her business that she hadn't thought of before, and she took it as a future thing she could try. Moral of the story: the story I had created in my head about the interaction and how she felt about me was not even real.

I learned a lesson at that moment. I learned I should stop assuming what people are thinking. I needed to stop making up stories in my head about things, because you know what happens when you assume right? I know you said it in your head right now, lol.

Back to the podcast episode—I was letting go of chasing people and forcing friendships.

There are two different types of relationships you can have with others: healthy ones and, well, UN-healthy ones.

Healthy ones look a lot like mutual respect, communication, shared interest in spending time together, support and trust, a healthy balance of giving and receiving at different times based on capacity, and also the respecting of that capacity, which is a big one. Healthy relationships look like feeling like you can speak freely without fear of abandonment from that friend, fear of judgment or repercussions from that partner (like not being worried that something you said isn't going to be thrown back in your face, or screenshotted and sent to someone else). A healthy relationship is when the other person respects your boundaries and honors them, they hold space for you, they share with you how much they care about you, and they mean it.

An unhealthy relationship is pretty much the opposite of everything I just said above. Someone who dismisses your feelings and tells you that you have no business feeling the way you do, not healthy. Someone who says one thing to you, but does the complete opposite, not healthy. Someone who makes you feel guilty for not spending time with them, not healthy. Someone who you worry will be mad at you if you cancel a plan with them because you need to take time for yourself, not healthy (this is what setting a boundary for yourself looks like and healthy friends will honor the shit out of that).

I will never forget the moment I realized I was making my way toward healthy friendships and was also honoring boundaries for myself. I love to share these moments with you, because my hope is that it gives you hope for what your squad could look like too!

A friend and I had made plans to get together after our young kids went to bed one night. She was a stay at home mom with 2 young kids, and at this time, I just had Clara. Well, the day came that we were supposed to get together and of course, with young kids, sometimes the day doesn't go the way you had wanted. The day ended up being jam packed, chaotic, and I hadn't gotten the chance to do my workout that day. I was working my way through a program, and I had made a commitment to myself that I was going to stick to that schedule and because of the way the day went, I wasn't going to be able to get that workout done until the evening, which was when I was supposed to get together with her. Early evening she sent me a message to confirm we were still on, and though it would have been really easy for me to bail on myself, especially because I wouldn't have wanted to upset her, I felt safe enough to respond to her by saying:

Today was wild and I actually didn't get the chance to move my body today. This is something that's really important to me, would you be okay with rescheduling?

My heart still raced as I hit send and waited for a reply because my desire to be liked programming is so deep, but she responded exactly how I had expected her to respond.

Good for you! Sorry your day was so crazy but I am totally cool with rescheduling. Enjoy your workout and let me know when you are free next.

Just like that, boundary set, boundary honored by a healthy friendship.

"A healthy relationship is when the other person respects your boundaries and honors them, they hold space for you, they share with you how much they care about you, and they mean it."

What would the current friends you have say to you in that situation?

Do you even feel like you could say this to your friends?

This is something I've had to work really hard at, and truthfully something I am still working through. Remember that friendship I had in high school?

There have been many situations where the same feelings come up from that day, and days before it, even if the situation is very different. Because the body and mind remember hard experiences, and the stories that came from these experiences have ingrained themselves deeply in our energetic blueprint, they can be unconsciously called up when triggered.

As I shared earlier, I've often found myself overcompensating in friendships and other relationships, just to make sure I never gave people a reason to not like me or to not want to spend time with me. I found myself being so envious of other women who I perceived to have it easy, those who were likeable and outgoing—the ones who always got invited to everything, the ones who I thought never had to feel like they weren't invited, because they always were. And because of these thoughts and feelings, I have always felt different. I often felt the weight of that story in the friendships I had. I felt the weight of it behind closed doors, in the room of my mind, never sharing it with others, because I was worried that if someone got to know the real me, the insecurities I had, what other people had done to me, that they wouldn't understand and that they would leave me too.

And it didn't feel good.

As I declared at the end of 2022, I needed to start to heal and release things like this.

One of the things that has been particularly helpful in my healing journey has been to find and nurture safe, predictable relationships and friendships. The biggest learning in this constant healing journey is that when you find the right people, the relationship flows naturally.

Whatever story you have about friendships and your worthiness and comfort in them, it's never too late. It's never too late for things to be different, and it's never too late to make a choice and choose you. Choosing you is true wellness and is true bliss.

And when you choose yourself, you ask for what you need, and you will never have to ask the right people to stay, because the people who are meant to be there, they just always will be.

Oh, and in case you were wondering, 2023 was the most incredible year filled with ease as it relates to friendships. When I stopped being worried about not being invited, wishing people wanted to spend more time with me, it allowed me to focus my energy on receiving from the new people that were becoming more present in my life.

It also allowed me to foster friendships that were already in place, allowing for new epic friendships to be made, and most importantly it took the looming pressure off friendships and changed some of them for the better. Less anxiety and more love.

Here are a few questions you can ask yourself as it relates to your relationships with others to help you do a little bit of an inventory. Think about a person (or people) in your life, and reflect on these questions:

Does thinking about this person make you feel light or heavy?

How do you feel after spending time with this person?

Does this relationship include a balance of give and take depending on where you are both at?

If you were struggling and needed support, would you feel safe to reach out to this person?

If given the choice, with no consequence/push back, would you move forward with the relationship?

If you are completely honest with yourself as you answer these, you will start to find the healthy and the unhealthy real quick.

Hit me up if you need some guidance on what to do with that, okay?

REFLECTION BLOCK
Self-Awareness & Inventory

When you think about your current friendships or relationships, what emotions come up first—peace, anxiety, joy, resentment, comfort, or something else?
Who in your life makes you feel *seen* and valued for who you are (not for what you do or give)?

CHAPTER 6

Your Emotions Deserve a Seat at the Table

And if you ask Clara, "They deserve to eat some spaghetti and meatballs."

I wrote this chapter as I overlooked the Three Sisters Mountains in Canmore on our girls' trip to Alberta. This was the first trip Clara and I had taken together. Just the two of us hopped on a plane and flew to Calgary to visit my sister—an adventure that years ago I would have never considered taking, because the anxiety of flying alone would have completely consumed me. I am pretty open about the fact that I have experienced feelings of anxiety most of my life, and traveling alone has been one of those things that has brought big emotions, ones that have felt so big, I all together avoided them. It's only been over the last couple of years that I have been overcoming the fear of travelling and getting on a plane, but I have only ever travelled with my "safe people" (do you have a person or two like that in your life?). I haven't flown anywhere by myself since I flew out to see my cousin in Thunder Bay when I was in highschool; that was the one and only time I have ever been on a plane solo. I've always been envious of people who can fly by themselves to places, or travel by themselves, because I've never been able to get over the anxious feelings that come along with even thinking about that. I'm still working through that one.

I experienced a lot of feelings on the trip to Canmore as I moved through nerves and discomfort, while simultaneously leaning into self-trust as I accomplished things I never thought I could. It was an emotional experience within myself both leading up to the trip as well as being on it.

I have to tell you something. It's big—are you ready? **In this chapter, I am going to bust the world's biggest kept secret.** Okay, I am being a little dramatic, but this is something I sure wish I would have learned sooner … it would have saved me many moments of shame, of frustration with myself, and it would have allowed me to come home to myself a bit sooner.

Here it goes …

Being emotional is NOT a weakness my friend. Ahh, there I said it. I'll say it again—having big feelings, heck, even having feelings, however they come up for you, is not a weakness. Having feelings doesn't make you dramatic, irrational, or ungrateful. It makes you a human. Emotions and feelings are a part of our genetic makeup, and whether they are positive or negative, they need to come out of your body or they build up over time, create stagnation, and then show up physically in other ways. They need to be expressed. Now, the way they show themselves is beautifully different for each of us, but all the ways they come out are right, NORMAL, and, especially if you are around me, welcomed. (I will add the caveat that feeling them and expressing them in healthy ways, and ways that don't harm others around you, is the key here, but we will get to that later.)

For so many years, I've felt big feelings about the fact that I have big feelings. I am a highly sensitive person, a feeler of the energies around me, and also a big feeler myself. I have been in numerous different types of situations throughout the course of my life where I have either felt like I was holding back tears, or where I have just cried, even when no one else is or even would be.

I am not kidding when I tell you:

When I feel happy, **I cry.**

When I feel sad, **I cry.**

When I feel angry, **I cry.**

When I feel overwhelmed, **I cry.**

When I feel pride, **I cry.**

When I feel almost anything, I feel the tears welling up inside of me. I felt like it made me seem weak, and I was embarrassed to be acting this way.

Somewhere along the way, probably in childhood and then definitely reinforced by society (THE STORRIEEESS), someone taught us that emotions are something to control, hide, or power through; some of us even learned to ignore them. Being emotional was wreckless, foolish, or immature, like you didn't have a handle on yourself, and that was something to feel ashamed about. Especially the heavy ones. Like, it's okay to be excited or happy, but the moment you get sad or angry? You better pull it together, bro.

I would like to offer you the idea of a new story, a different story: your emotions aren't the problem. Ignoring them is.

Let's take a minute to unpack why honoring your emotions—all of them, not just the "positive" ones—is one of the healthiest, most self-respecting things you can do, and on your journey to breaking free from all the things you SHOULD do, this is the next piece of that puzzle. Also, fun fact, when you allow yourself to have the fullest human experience, like feeling all the emotions, it's another great way to build that self-trust muscle.

So why do so many of us struggle with this in the first place? Do you? Or maybe just with some of them?

Many of us grew up in homes or cultures that considered emotions inconvenient, shameful, or even dangerous, unpredictable. We've also been conditioned by the media to believe this. Vulnerability and tears are seen as a weakness. I can think right now off the top of my head a few settings where crying is not acceptable and where showing anger/frustration (in a healthy way) would make people uncomfortable. In a business meeting, with your boss, at a professional event… all places I have cried at, for the record.

I use the example of crying often, because, in my experience, this is the one that most people have uncomfy feelings about showing or even seeing.

At an international retreat I recently hosted, as you would likely expect, there was an abundance of emotions and tears present, but you might be surprised to know just how often these women were apologizing for it. In a space that was safe and open to you showing up however you were, these women still felt shreds of shame for crying as we discussed things and brought things to the surface to be released. As if they had any control over this natural human response that we are often shamed for.

On the first day at the welcome party, one woman opened up so beautifully and emotionally while we were all sitting around the circle together. Afterwards when I checked in on her, she shared that she felt silly crying the way she did. She was worried people were going to think less of her and that they were judging her for having been so filled with so much emotion. Luckily, after self-reflection, she helped herself to realize her emotions were valid and that there is a place for them at the table. Now, imagine if she didn't have that insight. Imagine how many people are caught in the shame game, only to talk themselves out of ever showing emotion like that again and being open to being held and supported.

I bet you a time or two they've heard:

Stop crying, you're fine.

There's nothing to be upset about.

Why are you crying right now?

Are you seriously crying about this?

Nobody wants to hear you cry.

Any of these sound familiar?

These messages teach us that crying and emotions are bad and not welcomed. That they're something we need to shut down or suppress to be accepted. Pretending you're okay when you're not is seen as a strength and an accomplishment. That's not strength—it's emotional self-abandonment.

REFLECTION BLOCK

Your Emotions Blueprint

What did the family you grew up in teach you about emotions and feelings? Was it something you talked about? Was it something you didn't?

Think about the present when you spend time with your family ... Are emotions and feelings given space to be shared and felt? Or are they swept under the rug?

Spoiler Alert: your body doesn't care if you're trying to avoid your feelings. Whether you like it or not, they are going to come up, and you are going to have them exist in your body; it's the processing, or the lack thereof, that has its lasting effects on us.

Emotions are just energy in motion. They're not here to ruin your day (or your life, don't be dramatic) they're here to move *through* you. The more we try to stuff them down or pretend they don't exist, the more they get stuck. Most of the time, the only way past them is through them.

The Centre for Addiction and Mental Health (CAMH)—Canada's largest mental health hospital—has published countless studies showing how emotional suppression leads to higher rates of anxiety, depression, and even physical symptoms like chronic pain and insomnia.[12]

Emotional suppression happens when uncomfortable thoughts and feelings are pushed out of mind. We all do this in a variety of different ways, depending on what coping strategies we've developed over the years as we were living out other people's stories. Things like using distraction (i.e. watching TV), or numbing (through drugs and alcohol), to overeating or controlling food intake. Some of us channel emotions into physical activity (i.e. boxing, running, or going to the gym). Focusing our minds on something else helps us to forget what is really going on inside. There are many reasons people might consciously or sometimes unconsciously suppress emotions, too. It can be to avoid a big feeling that is socially unacceptable like rage, or to replace an uncomfortable feeling with a more acceptable or welcomed one. As we have already discussed a ton in this book, the expectations of other people in our lives influenced us a lot.[13]

When we don't express what's going on emotionally, that stress gets stored in our bodies, and the body keeps score. It piles up like unprocessed laundry in the back of our mind, like boxes in the storage locker that you don't want to deal with, but the weight of them is there and, eventually, it overflows. Maybe in a passive-aggressive comment. Maybe in burnout. Maybe in a sob session you didn't see coming.

When my dog passed away, I felt the most extreme sadness I have ever experienced in my life. Leading up to her passing, I was a wreck. After her passing, I was much the same. And I expressed it differently around different people in my life, based on how much sadness I thought I could show. Even though I know the importance of letting emotions flow.

But when I was alone in the safety of my home. I felt all of it. I allowed myself to sob. I allowed myself to exist and do absolutely nothing. I gave myself permission to feel it in all the ways I don't think I fully ever gave myself permission before.

"Pretending you're okay when you're not is seen as a strength and an accomplishment. That's not strength—it's emotional self-abandonment."

I remember when we got home from the vet office, I came right upstairs and stood there for a minute, staring at her dog bed. It was scary the amount of sorrow that was consuming me in that moment, but instead of pushing it down to "get on with my day" I allowed it to take me to my knees and fall over onto her bed. There I was, alone in the bedroom, weeping into the fabric. Some time passed and it eventually subsided and slowed down, but imagine how bottled up that grief would have been in my body if I didn't just let it flow, despite the fear of how long it might last. I gave it space, and it moved through me.

Feeling is FREEING!

I'm not kidding when I say it changed everything for me when I realized and leaned into the fact that emotions don't need to simply be fixed. They need to be felt.

I am now regularly known to need a good cry to release, and now that I know how much it helps me, I just lean all the way in. Sometimes, depending on the day, my husband notices my need and holds me a little longer, giving me space to cry (usually soaking his t-shirt). Then, when I'm done, I feel so much better!

Let's say you're feeling frustrated. The go-to reaction might be: *Ugh, I shouldn't feel this way. I have nothing to complain about.* But that kind of thinking just shuts the door on what's really going on and the validity of that emotion for coming up.

What if you just got curious instead? Just noticed it, sat with it for a moment and then gave yourself space to explore why it might come up?

"I like to think of emotions like weather patterns. They roll in, they peak, and then they pass—if we let them."

You could use statements like:

I'm feeling frustrated right now. What's that about?

This situation doesn't sit well with me. That's okay.
I wonder why?

I don't have to fix this feeling—I can just feel it.

This concept is less about spiraling and staying stuck and wallowing ... It's more about being emotionally honest and listening to yourself, which is something that doesn't always come naturally to us. It's definitely a skill to be learned, but feeling your feelings gives you more regulation, and more control. Not less.

I like to think of emotions like weather patterns. They roll in, they peak, and then they pass—if we let them. But most of us are out here trying to micromanage the damn weather. We tell ourselves to "get over it" or "just think happy thoughts," and meanwhile the storm just gets louder.

Side note: for as long as I can remember, I've hated thunderstorms. Any sort of unstable weather would send me into an anxious mess. My friend and I often text each other when there was an impending storm exchanging our wishes for it to just be gone. She's my thunder buddy.

But now, though I am not going to make a declaration that I love them, I don't mind them the same way I used to. I now have the approach of just letting them roll through and be. I wonder if there is something there ...

When you give yourself permission to feel what you're feeling, it often passes faster. This is such a cool way to honor yourself. You deserve to feel the comfort that comes when you've moved through those emotions, especially the tough ones. And the way you move through them is different, so when you're open to it, it's also a way to learn more about yourself, too. You can learn the different ways your body feels different emotions and how it feels to live in the calm that comes after it.

Recently, my daughter was getting ready to head to the airport with her dad. They were going on a trip out west to visit her grandparents. It was the first time she had taken a flight without me, and as it got closer to the time they were leaving, she was feeling some feelings about it. I could tell the nerves were building for her because she was getting more quiet and she was becoming short with me when I was making sure she had everything she needed. I've been really intentional in teaching her about feeling into her emotions and reminding her to give herself the space to feel them, so I took this as an opportunity to have her tune in.

I told her I noticed she was a bit more quiet, and I asked her if she was okay. She told me she was feeling nervous and that she didn't want to go. (Gosh, how many of us have avoided people, and situations because we didn't like the feelings that came along with them?) We talked about how what she was feeling was super normal, and I even told her I often felt this way before leaving the house, especially if I was going on a trip without her and her sister. We also talked about how these feelings rarely last. I gave her the example of over-whelming joy and happiness—we often feel those feelings in the moment when things are happening, and then that feeling fades. I explained to her that unwanted feelings were much the same. When we're feeling the unwanted feelings, it's easy to get caught up in the thought that they might last forever, which causes our anxiety to be even greater, but these feelings fade and subside, just like the happy ones do.

That conversation made her feel a lot more calm, and since then she's used this mini pep talk with herself as well. It was a great learning opportunity for her and a great reminder for all of us.

If you've ever had a stress stomachache, a tight jaw from anger, or that post-anxiety exhaustion where you feel you ran a marathon? Listen in, that's likely your body telling you: *Hey babe, I'm feeling this with you. Let's move through it so we can move on.*

Okay, we've talked a lot about why this matters. But what does this actually look like in your real, everyday life?

You know I love me some good real-life examples of how you can apply this, or how it might show up, so here are a few examples:

You feel overwhelmed, but keep pushing through your day.

Instead of spiraling into guilt or self-blame, you pause. You say to yourself: *I'm feeling maxed out. I need to take a breath.* You step outside for 5 minutes. You cry in your car if you need to. You honor the overwhelm instead of shaming it.

You feel angry about something small (like someone cutting you off in traffic).

Instead of calling yourself dramatic, you get curious. *Am I really just angry about this moment? Or am I carrying something deeper?* Maybe it's resentment, stress, or feeling underappreciated. Boom—you just connected to the actual feeling underneath.

You notice a tight chest or shallow breathing.

This is one that happens often for me, and historically, I would panic immediately. I would be so nervous that I was anxious again because I felt out of control in those moments with such a big disconnection from what was going on and how to regulate it. Over the years, I have learned that this is the time I need to pause. Instead of spiraling and getting overwhelmed, this is the moment where I need to ask myself, *What emotion might be in my body right now?* And by taking some time to do a bit of a body and mind scan, I can usually pin point pretty quickly what's going on and why I am feeling it, and then I can move through it.

It can be that simple. You tune in. You listen. You honor it with no need to fix it.

This doesn't require an entire therapy session every time you get activated, either. It's more about micro-moments of honesty and checking in ... like checking in with yourself instead of checking out.

You deserve to be seen—especially by yourself.

You deserve to be witnessed—especially by you.

That means allowing your sadness to exist. Your anger to be acknowledged. Your grief to take up space. Your joy to expand without shrinking it down to be "palatable."

We are emotional creatures and quite frankly, trying to live like we're robots with productivity goals and hustle culture is killing our nervous systems and our self-worth. This is a plea for grace for yourself. You deserve more.

"We are emotional creatures and quite frankly, trying to live like we're robots with productivity goals and hustle culture is killing our nervous systems and our self-worth. This is a plea for grace for yourself. You deserve more."

Girlfriend, let yourself be a full-ass human. Feel the big feelings. Cry when the moment calls for it. Laugh so hard you snort. Get angry. Get excited. **Feel everything.**

Because every emotion you have is valid. Every feeling has a place. And every time you honor your emotions, you come home to yourself a little more.

If you've spent years—or decades—not feeling safe to express your emotions, this chapter might feel kind of tender. It's like a truth you've always known but weren't allowed to express openly.

You're allowed to feel everything.

You're allowed to not have it all together.

You're allowed to be a beautiful, emotional, raw, growing work in progress.

And in case no one's told you lately, that's enough. Feeling your feelings isn't a weakness. It's wisdom. And you, you're allowed to be wise and messy all at the same time.

REFLECTION BLOCK
Emotional Compassion

If you spoke to yourself about your emotions the way you would to someone you love, what would you say to them?

How can you integrate that compassion into your daily life?

CHAPTER 7

Boundaries are Loving Yourself Out Loud

"Daring to set boundaries is about having the courage to love ourselves, even when we risk disappointing others."
- Brené Brown

I don't know about you, but I never learned about boundaries.

I never remember it being touched on when I was in college, and it certainly wasn't anything we ever discussed in high school or elementary school, so for the longest time I never even knew what a boundary was. Until I did. And now, I can't imagine my life without them. After this chapter, that might be you, too. I sure hope so!

Let me explain.

Have you ever seen the movie Wine Country? It's quite funny. If you haven't, take a moment to add it to your must-watch list (you're welcome).

There's this one scene where they're all out for dinner, and across the restaurant, they spot Brené Brown sitting in a booth with her friends. She's just enjoying a night out, socially of course, not in "work mode." Some of the girls in the group are totally fangirling. The others, oddly, don't really know who she is (I still can't believe that part, but I digress lol). The ones who recognize her are buzzing, throwing around their favorite quotes and takeaways from her work. You can tell how much she's resonated with them.

So naturally, they decide to go over to her table. They want to tell her how much they love her work, and ask a few questions, and about thirty seconds into approaching her—while they're mid-gush—she gently but firmly interrupts, says something about "boundaries," draws an invisible circle around her table, and says it again.

Boundaries.

She doesn't raise her voice. She doesn't excessively explain herself. Instead she just lets that word land, and then quietly returns to her friends. The group suddenly gets the message and slowly backs away, honoring it in every sense of the word to how she proclaimed it.

And honestly? I thought that moment was a badass.

Her behavior wasn't rude. She was being real, and in that moment, she honored her needs and showed up for herself by asking for it. It was apparent she'd made a decision that when she's out socially with her people and her friends, that it's a sacred time. Not a "let me fix your life" time. And she didn't care if anyone felt uncomfortable about it. She respected herself too much not to hold firm in the line she created.

That scene stayed with me. Probably because, back then, I couldn't even imagine doing that.

"It's also likely that your boundaries will change over the course of your life as you learn more about yourself, grow, and possibly shift your priorities as well as how you move through the milestones of life."

What Even Are Boundaries?

A very simple definition of boundaries is that they are the lines and limits you create between yourself and other people. They allow you to define what is acceptable and healthy for you in your relationships. The boundaries you communicate and maintain can protect you both physically and psychologically. They also protect your time energy, which is your biggest currency and should be guarded and given wisely.[14]

The beauty of life and the uniqueness in humans is that everyone has different values, needs, and sensitivities, so defining personal boundaries varies from person to person. It's also likely that your boundaries will change over the course of your life as you learn more about yourself, grow, and possibly shift your priorities as well as how you move through the milestones of life. I know mine have gotten real tight since becoming a parent for the second time, with how busy we are in this season and with how important family time is to me.

If you're reading this book, you may have done a little self-development work already, so maybe this isn't the first time you've heard about boundaries. (And if it is, I am EXTRA excited you've taken the time to read it this far!) The real question is though: are you actually living them? Are you practicing them? Are you sharing them and are you honoring them?

Because knowing about boundaries and holding boundaries are two very different things, lemme tell ya! Holding them in the complexities of relationships and the life circumstances and the seasons is not for the faint of heart.

For a long time, I wasn't doing either.

For most of my life, I teetered on people-pleasing. I grew up keeping the peace, never wanting to put anyone out. I was always the one being there for people, and god forbid someone was mad at me or didn't like me, I would be crushed! I struggled with a deep fear of abandonment. That fear didn't just show up one day though, it was a reaction to things I'd experienced in my childhood and teenage years, like it is for most of us, and somewhere along the line I absorbed the message that if I was just good enough, agreeable enough, low-maintenance enough, maybe people wouldn't leave.

So I overcompensated.

In friendships, I was always the one saying yes. In relationships, I bent over backwards to be liked. I didn't speak up when something hurt me or made me uncomfortable. I confused "being easy going" with "never having needs." I said yes when I wanted to say no and then silently resented people for not reading my mind.

Sound familiar?

I still remember some of the first times I had to take the concept of boundaries out of the podcast episodes and books I was learning from and actually use them in real life with real people I knew and loved and was living life with. Let me tell you, it made me *sweat.* Literally. Like, heart-racing, stomach-in-knots, *maybe I'll just let it go this time* kind of sweat. And if you're wondering, yes I did indeed let it go for much longer than I should have.

One example that comes to mind was with a close family member. And I use this story because, let's be honest—so often it *is* family, or those close, long-standing relationships, where boundaries feel the hardest to speak up about or to implement. It feels hard because it's not just about managing your own energy and your own feelings around needing to speak up, it's about managing your emotions AND theirs. You care about them. You don't want to offend them or hurt their feelings. You don't want to make them feel unwelcome or push them away (this is of course if you are still wanting to maintain a relationship with them … putting up boundaries to reduce or remove access to your life is a totally different story) and so that adds this heavy emotional weight to something that seems so simple when I write it to you here on paper. I get that.

This person, who I love very much, had a habit of dropping by our house unannounced. Like, no text, just a knock at the door because they were in the area or had something to drop off or wanted to see the kids. And that's what made it so hard for me at first because I knew this was coming from a place of love, I got it, they love the kids, they were being kind and spontaneous just to spend some extra time with us. But I'm a mom managing all the mom things and all the schedules. I work, I run a household, and I value my sacred space and sacred time with my family. The unpredictability of it was draining for me. It would be challenging on the days where we had things going on, or had HAD a busy day and I was just wanting to do nothing. Even if I wasn't busy, I'd feel like I had to drop everything and host, and most of the time I would. And then I found myself being frustrated at the situation, frustrated with them, and then I'd be annoyed with myself for doing it *again*.

And so because of all of that, like I said, I let it go for a bit. I told myself I was being dramatic and that it wasn't a big deal. That I should just be grateful to have this family member, but each time it happened, it chipped away at me. And eventually, I realized I needed to speak up even though it made me wildly uncomfortable, because it had the potential to damage the relationship with the building resentment that was happening.

I spent days rehearsing what I'd say. Literally played it over in my head like a movie. I wanted to be kind but firm. I didn't want it to come off as rude or cold, because that's not the intention for this conversation, and like I said before, I really cared about this relationship. And girl, when the time came to say something in the moment, my voice shook. My palms were sweaty, my knees felt weak (my arms were heavy). But I said it. I told them how much we loved seeing them, but that I really appreciated a heads-up before any visits, so I could make sure we were available and not in the middle of something. I made every effort to make sure they understood the intention was about mutual respect—respecting our schedule, our rhythm, and my own energy as a parent and a person.

They were surprised at first, of course. I wouldn't expect them to react any differently! (Hence why I avoided it for 2343639285734596 years.) It even wasn't so well received initially. Which I would like to note is also normal. Things changing can throw us for a loop, having hard conversations isn't always easy at first, though it does get easier with practice, and I was establishing a thread of conversation and a topic that wasn't really something that had been a part of the dynamic of our relationship before. It was new, and it was awkward. It was hard, but the world didn't end, and the relationship didn't crumble.

Slowly, things started to shift and to get better. They started texting first. They asked what times worked best. And I noticed that I showed up better when we did hang out, I wasn't secretly annoyed or drained or overwhelmed. I was present. I was warm. I had made space for myself and that allowed me to show up more authentically with them.

That small sweat-worthy decision cracked something open for me. It made me realize just how often we're showing up in our lives with this low-level tension under the surface feeling frustrated or overwhelmed or feeling like our energy is being pulled in too many directions, but we smile through it because we think that's what we should do. Especially when it comes to people we love. We think that loving them means always being available. Always saying yes. Always keeping the peace. But when you're constantly abandoning yourself to make others comfortable, you're not actually connecting. You're performing. You're pretending. And that's not love—that's burnout in disguise.

Setting that one boundary reminded me I deserve to feel safe and respected in my own space. I'm allowed to have needs, and those needs don't make me selfish or difficult or dramatic. They make me human. And when I honored that—when I made space for myself instead of pushing myself aside—what came through was so much better.

> **REFLECTION BLOCK**
>
> **Where Am I Saying Yes When I Want to Say No?**
>
> Take 10 minutes to write down areas of your life where you often say "yes" out of guilt, fear, or habit. (relationships, work, family) For each, ask yourself:
> What would it feel like to say no? What am I afraid might happen if I do? This will help you notice wherea boundary might bring more peace.

It's wild how something so small saying, Hey, *can you text before you come by?* shifted the foundation of how I have lived going forward since that moment. It built self-trust. It built confidence. It rippled into reminding me that I didn't have to twist myself into a thousand different shapes to be loved. I just had to be truthful, truthful to myself. And that honesty, even when it's scary, is what creates space for the real connection we're all craving.

Boundaries don't push the right people away. They give you the space to show up more fully, which makes your relationships deeper, stronger, and more real. They help us stay connected in ways that feel safe and sustainable. They let us show up as our full selves, without resentment bubbling underneath the surface. And most of all, they show the people in our lives how to love us in the way we actually need to be loved.

I need to make this clear again one more time, doing this WAS NOT EASY ... and did not come naturally, like at all.

"**Boundaries don't push the right people away. They give you the space to show up more fully, which makes your relationships deeper, stronger, and more real.**"

Before this practice (and other situations), boundaries felt like this scary, foreign concept to me like something only really confident, unbothered people knew how to do. I genuinely believed that if I started setting boundaries, I would lose people. They'd think I was difficult or selfish or asking for too much. I was worried I would no longer be liked, which is a pretty old story, and one I don't like to give fuel to. Over time though, I realized that every time I abandoned myself to keep someone else comfortable, I was deepening my own wound, and that I ultimately couldn't control the outcome of the situation anyway. I was scared. I was scared of pushing people away and being left with no one.

And as I learned more about the reason for boundaries and what their intended purpose is, it increased my comfort in using them and speaking my truth. The purpose of boundaries isn't to push people away ... not at all. They are not walls that we build around us, they are bridges to keep us connected. They're how we teach people how to love and respect us. Without them, resentment grows. Communication breaks down. We feel used, exhausted, misunderstood (you name it), and then we blame the people around us for not getting us or for not respecting us. Most of the time, we just haven't shared with them what feels okay with us and what doesn't. We just assume they should know and then we feel frustrated when they don't. The biggest flex in life is sharing with people what our limits are and how we would like to be interacted with and treated ... because usually they honestly just don't know.

Boundaries aren't about shutting people out, they're about letting the right people in, in a way that feels safe, honoring, and mutual. Especially if you've spent years being the "yes girl," the helper, the fixer, the "I've got it!" friend, the one who always shows up no matter what. (It's me, hi!) People get used to that version of you. So when you shift—even slightly—they notice. And sometimes, they push back. Which is why boundaries can be so fucking hard at first—that oftentimes we say forget it. It's just easier this [old] way.

Not everyone is going to cheer you on when you set a boundary and that can be really uncomfortable, too. Learning to sit with the feeling of someone being disappointed in you without rushing to fix it is a muscle to be built, a skill to be crafted ... but it's also part of becoming the kind of woman who embodies bliss, a woman who doesn't just talk about self-love but actually lives it.

Okay.

So no.

No. No.

Say it with me ... "NO."

Saying no is a boundary. Saying no is a full sentence.

You don't owe people long-winded explanations. You don't have to make excuses. And you don't need to apologize for needing time, space, rest, or peace.

Here's a little list of permission slips and things I lean into, in case you need some (I LOVEEE A GOOD PERMISSION SLIP!):

You're allowed to say no to events, even if you don't have anything else going on.

You're allowed to not reply to that text until tomorrow and to know that people aren't going to be mad at you for it.

You're allowed to leave early.

You're allowed to change your mind.

You're allowed to not take the call.

You're allowed to unfollow or unfriend anyone whose energy drains you.

You're allowed to ask for what you need.

And you're allowed to do all of that without guilt.

Having boundaries and saying no doesn't make you mean, my friend. There's a way to speak your truth and ask for what you need in a respectful way. (That, and we can't control other people either so we aren't responsible for how they react or perceive us.) But this is the fear so many women that I speak with have.

They think that if they start asserting themselves, there is a chance that they might come across as cold or selfish or even rude. Girlfriend, boundaries are an act of kindness—not just for us, but for the people in our lives. When we're clear about what works for us and what doesn't, we show up more authentically. Our relationships become more real. We stop pretending. We create space for mutual respect. It is so freeing to be around people who get you, honor you, and don't expect you to burn yourself out to keep them happy.

I am not saying I went out there one day and started boundary-ing all over everyone in my life. I built the muscle by starting small with people where it felt safe. I set the boundary, HELD MY BREATH, and waited for the response. When it was honored, it helped me to practice for the situations in which they might not be. And when they aren't honored, I stand firm in knowing that it's not about me, it's about them … and it certainly doesn't mean that I should go back on what I said. Instead, I make a mental note of how that went, and allow it to inform how I move forward in situations with that person. I am always learning about the people in my life and also about myself as I evolve into new versions of myself—and as I evolve, I keep practicing!

REFLECTION BLOCK
The Boundary Challenge

Think of a situation where you could practice setting a boundary this week.

Write down:

How you'll communicate it and then do it. Afterward, reflect: *How did it feel to honor myself?*

When you begin honoring your own boundaries, you don't just give yourself a better experience of life—you also show others what might be possible for them. You start to show them what it looks like to choose yourself without guilt. You teach them that it's safe to listen to their body, to their gut, to their spirit, and you can take it one step further by becoming the kind of person who holds space for others to do the same. I've watched this play out in my own life, and it's so super cool.

I remember I was asking a friend if she wanted to get together one week; it had been a while since we'd seen each other, and we were just talking about how we missed each other.

"When you become the kind of person who welcomes boundaries instead of resisting them, you contribute to a new way of relating. You become the example of what's possible in friendship, in community, and in love."

When I asked her about getting together, she paused, and then she said, "As much as I would love to say yes, I think I need to just chill after running so much." I smile just thinking about this because I KNOW that answer was hard for her!

I told her "OF COURSE!" I told her I was proud of her for listening to herself, and saying that even when it was hard. And I kid you not, she's talked about that exchange multiple times since then to our friends, and how much that meant for her.

You get to be the safe space for others too.

Safe space doesn't mean you have to agree with or fully understand someone's boundary, but it does mean that you choose to honor it anyway. You don't question it. You don't guilt-trip it. You don't make it about you. You support it because you know how brave it can be to set a boundary in the first place.

We all want to feel free to say, *This is what I need right now,* and be met with grace instead of resistance. You have the power to be that grace. You have the power to normalize that level of self-honoring in your circle.

YOU get to be THAT friend.

Be the friend who doesn't give your friend a hard time when she just needs to stay home.

Be the friend who lets her leave the party early without teasing her or calling her "boring."

Be the friend who encourages her to follow her gut, even if it means canceling plans, changing her mind, or disappointing you. (The frequency to which a friend keeps not showing up to you and feels very one sided is a separate conversation and not about honoring boundaries.)

Be the friend who doesn't pressure her to have a drink, stay out later, or push past what feels good for her.

Be the friend who listens with curiosity—not defensiveness—when she says, *That comment didn't land well for me.*

Be the friend who supports her eating choices without making her explain them.

Be the friend who doesn't take it personally when she says no to your invitation.

Be the friend who asks, *What would feel supportive right now?* instead of assuming you know.

Be the friend who understands that just because someone says yes once doesn't mean they owe you a yes every time.

Be the friend who celebrates someone saying no—not because it benefits you, but because it means they're honoring themselves.

This is what emotional safety looks like.

This is what it means to practice boundary culture.

When you become the kind of person who welcomes boundaries instead of resisting them, you contribute to a new way of relating. You become the example of what's possible in friendship, in community, and in love. Most people just need to know that it's safe and welcomed for them to be real.

Safe to change their minds. Safe to say *no.* Safe to say *yes* to themselves. Safe to honor what they're feeling. Safe to not have to explain why. You can be that safe space, and in doing so, you don't just create deeper connections—you create liberation.

I will end with this, boundaries aren't something you learn once and then master forever. They're a daily practice. A muscle you build. And the more you flex it, the stronger it gets. Sometimes it'll feel easy. Other times you'll stumble and people-please out of habit. That's okay. Give yourself grace. Then try again. But I promise you that when you start setting boundaries, you stop betraying yourself. You stop living from a place of obligation and start living from a place of alignment.

And that's what this journey is really about.

I'll leave you with this:

"The only people who get upset about you setting boundaries are the ones who were benefiting from you not having any."

Let that sink in.

You're not too much. You're not selfish. You're just finally choosing you.

Where in your life are you saying YES when you really want to be saying no?

CHAPTER 8

Return to Joy, Play, and Laughing Until You Pee Your Pants

On a scale of 1 to 10, how much joy are you actually feeling in your life right now? (Remember what I said about awareness being key?) Don't overthink it—just gut-check it. How would you answer that question without thinking about it for more than 5 seconds?

Are you coasting at 5?

Floating at a solid 8?

Or hanging on somewhere around 2 and pretending it's fine?

That number, whatever it is, isn't about judgment. We're just taking a minute to gather data. This will help to give a snapshot of where you are—and more importantly, how much space there might be in your soul to create more lightness, more laughter, more moments that feel good instead of just "fine." That's what we're going to spend this entire chapter chatting about!

"Your inner child carries all of that, the innocence, the wonder, the hurt, the hope, and even though you've grown up, they never stopped existing. They're there beneath the surface, influencing how you react, how you love, how you protect yourself, and how you see the world."

Contrary to what you may have learned, or what others led you to believe growing up, joy and play are not the luxuries of life reserved for certain people, and not for certain ages, these things are for EVERYONE (yes girl, even you!). They're essential parts of a full life. Joy and play ease our stress, help us rediscover ourselves amid the busyness, and remind us that life isn't only about a never-ending to-do list. It deeply connects us to our inner child and honors their needs.

Have you heard the term *inner child* before? It's one of those phrases that gets used often in the self-growth world, but it's really simple—your inner child is the younger version of you that still lives within you today, and everyone has one, whether it's acknowledged or not. It's the part of you that holds your earliest memories, emotions, dreams, and even your wounds. The one who learned what love felt like (or didn't), who discovered how to get attention or stay safe, who absorbed messages about what made her "good," "enough," or "too much." A lot of the things we've already discussed in this book were absorbed by your inner child when they first were exposed to it, and that's who created the stories. Your inner child carries all of that, the innocence, the wonder, the hurt, the hope, and even though you've grown up, they never stopped existing. They're there beneath the surface, influencing how you react, how you love, how you protect yourself, and how you see the world.

I remember listening to a Mel Robbins podcast episode one time, and she said that every big reaction you see from a grown up is just their inner 8-year-old showing up, and that's why sometimes reactions are big, emotional, and don't make sense. It's because our inner child is reacting or being triggered in that situation—this is true for all of us.

Honoring your inner child is just *healing* the parts of you that learned the story to dim your light to fit in. It's about giving love, safety, and compassion to the version of you who didn't always get it. It's wild when you start to understand that when we don't pay attention to our wounded inner child, we often repeat the same patterns they learned like people-pleasing, fear of rejection, overachieving to feel worthy, or shutting down when things feel too big. But when we honor them? Everything shifts.

You start giving yourself permission to play again, but also to rest. To create just because it feels good. You stop hustling for love and start realizing you already deserve it and that it can also come from within you.

REFLECTION BLOCK
Meeting Your Inner Child

If you were to picture your inner child, how old are they?
What are they doing? What emotions do they carry—joy, sadness, curiosity, fear, hope?
What would they tell you about the stories they have?

The problem is that in our grown up lives, we spend so much time managing, fixing, and achieving that sometimes we forget we're allowed, actually designed, to feel good. We're allowed to laugh until our stomachs hurt, to move for the fun of it, not just for exercise points, and we're allowed to be silly, goofy, and childish even though we have, like, a mortgage and shit. Returning to joy is a coming home. It can be what helps make life feel worth living, not just worth surviving.

A couple years ago, my friend shared a funny Amazon review on her social media. The review was for a viral dress on TikTok that apparently no matter your body type you could put it on and you would look great and feel an increased sense of confidence about yourself. I'm literally giggling as I write this—the review shared that the dress did not disappoint.

The review went a little something like this:

Buy it. At the very moment I was trying on this dress, my house CAUGHT FIRE!! I ran around trying to get my kids out, and wasn't thinking about the fact that I was wearing this dress. I fell 3 times running back and forth. lol I tweaked my ankle and skinned my knees, but this dress held up! When the firefighters got here, I looked AMAZING and I think they noticed. Amazon dress for the win. I went back and bought them all.

It's almost embarrassing to tell you HOW MANY TIMES I read this review over and over. You would think that after a while the hilarity would have worn off, but I was laughing the same amount every time, if not more, unable to breathe because this review was something I just couldn't get over. Some people might read it and wonder how the heck it was funny, or not find it funny at all. But man, it was a glorious moment for me. My body, my cells, and my brain were loving it.

I love to do this and frequently do with movies or anything that I am watching. It's not uncommon for me to rewind it, or watch something over and over again when a funny part shows up. It usually gets me laughing more and more each time. My husband has recorded me doing this a couple times, maybe because he thinks I am ridiculous (though it gets him laughing too) but gosh, it makes me feel so good!

Do you remember what it was like to be a child? (I know that might feel really far away to you.)

If that feels hard to picture or maybe you would prefer to not go back there then perhaps this is a better question: do you spend a lot of time around children?

If you do, you might notice they spend so much of their days laughing! And it's likely that when you're around them, you are more jovial at seemingly small things. They will laugh at anything, and they laugh often. Did you know the average 4-year-old laughs 300 times a day?! Want to take a guess at how many times the average 40-year-old laughs?

I'll wait.

4. 4 times. PER DAY.[15] This was the one stat that got me the most while writing this book. The number of adults not fully enjoying life as is biologically needed really bums me out.

REFLECTION BLOCK
Awareness Before Action

When was the last time you felt genuinely light, carefree, or playful? What were you doing, and who were you with? What might be getting in the way of allowing yourself to feel that more often?

One of my favorite things to watch as a kid was *America's Funniest Home Videos*. I've been through Bob Saget, Carlton from Fresh Prince, and Tom Burgeron, and through all of them, the videos never failed to deliver senseless laughter. I loved it. It was such a simpler time in my life. Your life was probably simpler too at one time, but then we grew up.

I don't know the exact age or the time, but at some point we're fed the story that it's time to get serious. It's time to stop "messing around" and to grow up. We laugh, like really laugh less, and we play less. There's less safety and encouragement to find joy. Overall, we enjoy the simplicity of life less. Life gets more serious, we experience more stressors, more pressures, more responsibility, and as a result, we give ourselves less opportunity to play, to be creative and lighthearted, because it's seen as childish and immature or not something we should prioritize. It's often even considered foolish if we prioritize this over the "grown-up things" we have to do. So then, we go through our days living through all the pressures, all the roles we have and suddenly weeks or months have gone by since we've laughed. And then we wonder why we're feeling so off, so stressed and so *not like ourselves*, it's because we haven't had our release, and we haven't given ourselves the opportunity for this simple medicine of life.

Laughter and play are so good for us, and they can mean everything when it comes to living a life of more happiness.

Studies and articles say so, okay!

Have you ever heard the statement, *Laughter is the best medicine*? Laughing literally has quantifiable psychological and physiological side effects. When you have a good and fulfilling belly laugh, or you laugh until you can't breathe, can't talk, and you cry (that is my favorite) you are actually releasing physical tension and stress in your muscles, and the effects from that good laugh can last in your body for up to 45 minutes.[16]

Tell me you've experienced this? Can you think about when the last time was?

Laughing elevates your mood because it releases endorphins—the feel-good chemicals. Like exercise does. Cue the *Legally Blonde* reference here: *Exercise releases endorphins, endorphins make you happy, happy people just don't kill their husbands.* So, when laughing, you often get that natural high and boost from a simple (childish) activity.

Besides elevating your mood by releasing endorphins, and reducing feelings of stress, there is some really cool research that came out of a study conducted in Maryland in 2006.

Scientists at the University of Maryland School of Medicine discovered a fascinating connection between laughter and heart health. They found that when we laugh, the inner lining of our blood vessels actually expand to increase blood flow. Bodies are so cool. On the flip side though, stress causes those same blood vessels to constrict and reduce blood flow. A professor of medicine and the lead researcher said the idea to study the effects of positive emotions like laughter came after they noticed how mental stress made blood vessels tighten up.

In one of their studies, the volunteers watched a movie that made them laugh one day and scenes from a war documentary the next day. They took over 300 measurements throughout the study, and when the volunteers watched the stressful movie, their blood vessels constricted, which lined up with previous studies showing that mental stress narrows blood vessels.

But here's the fun part: when they watched the comedy and were laughing, their blood vessels expanded! They pointed out that the changes they saw in the inner lining of the blood vessels, from laughing, were like the benefits you'd get from aerobic exercise. So, in a nutshell, laughing more might just help us keep heart disease at bay![17]

This is just an example of one benefit, but just in case you needed more, here's a summary list for you because I really want us to see how MANY benefits come from this simple, easy, and free support for your body!

What are the physical, mental, and social benefits of laughter?

Physical health benefits	**Mental health benefits**	**Social benefits**
• Boosts immunity	• Adds joy and zest to life	• Strengthens relationships
• Lowers stress hormones	• Eases anxiety and tension	• Attracts others to us
• Decreases pain	• Relieves stress	• Enhances teamwork
• Relaxes your muscles	• Improves mood	• Helps defuse conflict
• Prevents heart disease	• Strengthens resilience	• Promotes group bonding

2024 was the hardest year of my life. After just having realized at the end of 2023 that I was experiencing burnout (which I was learning more about trying to heal from), we received news that rocked our family to its core.

It was November 2023. I still remember sitting at the kitchen table, working, when my husband came home and told me that his company was completely out of money. My heart sank. All the blood drained from my face—I had no words. How could this happen? What does this even mean for our family? I was terrified, but I didn't want to show it because I could only imagine the way he was feeling by the look on his face.

Over the next few months, we would come to discover that his business partner had a gambling addiction and the company had secretly been feeding his habit without us knowing it—in a big way. We discovered that over the course of 4 years he had taken $500,000, replacing it in small amounts and then taking it again, depending on the frequency of the gambling and personal spending. It was devastating to learn that a company that was the legacy of our family and the thing my husband had spent 10 years building, his dream, was shattered.

It took a significant toll on our family, on me, and on our relationship. I am giving you no bullshit when I tell you we barely made it through that year. There was no fun and no lightness in our lives. Everything was so heavy all the time, and we were exhausted. There was very little joy. On top of everything we were navigating with the business and what that meant for us, how we were going to move forward, we had to say goodbye to our family dog.

"I didn't realize it at the time, but I was slowly healing my nervous system. Doing intentional activities like that allows time for your body to rest on a cellular level—it's comparable to meditation."

She had been with us throughout our entire marriage. She was our first child, and when she got hurt in the summer of 2024, it made the cloud over us even heavier. In October of that year, when we finally had to let her go—she was approaching her 11th birthday, and it was devastating to us all.

I think back to that year and truly feel like I barely made it.

During what was the hardest year of our lives and of my life, I knew I needed to find ways to cope and to manage. And while I was actively in therapy, between recovering from the burnout and dealing with everything that life was giving us, I needed an outlet. This was right around the time I made the first bead bracelet I had made in a very long time—honestly, since I was a child. I was at a friend's house for a hangout when she pulled out her bead collection while we were catching up. I made a bracelet for the first time in my adult life, and I found joy in that small, simple activity. I left there knowing I needed to incorporate it as part of my life at home. One thing I had been doing to recover from my burnout was making sure I kept my evenings open to just *be*, and to just *exist* with my kids and my family. Having a business meant that I had worked a lot in the evenings, and I was actively trying to move away from that so I could find myself again. So, when I say I needed to incorporate that into my life ... I really got into bracelets.

Shortly after that hangout, I started my own bead collection. I bought myself a small kit at first, and I started making bracelets in the evenings. I would make them by myself, with other friends (I was that person bringing beads to all the girls' nights), and I was also making them with my older daughter. Shortly after that, I bought more. Perhaps more than a grown adult woman *should* buy, but I did because it was fun. It was a fun thing that we could do together, and more than that, it became an intentional focused time where I could just be me. I tuned in and allowed myself to do something for fun that was for absolutely nothing else. There was no strategy behind it, there was no ROI, it would not propel my business forward. None of that. And if I am being really honest, because that's what we are here to do, it was the first time I had done something like that as an adult. I didn't realize it at the time, but I was slowly healing my nervous system. Doing intentional activities like that allows time for your body to rest on a cellular level—it's comparable to meditation.

I also started collecting stickers and organizing a sticker book!

My daughters got stickers and a sticker book for their birthdays that year, and it excited the little girl within me. I wished at that moment that someone would get ME stickers so I could organize them! I remembered I had a pink hardcover sticker book when I was a kid, and I had filled it with the most random stickers I got because as a kid, I loved stickers! It was so fun.

When did I stop collecting stickers? Probably when the world told me to.

I was now a grown up, with all my grown up money and access to the best stickers that money could buy! So, I got myself a sticker book with a ton of stickers, and I was giddy when they showed up at my house. The 8-year-old in me felt so seen and taken care of. I found stickers with cute sayings, stickers that were pretty, stickers that were fun, stickers that were witchy, and stickers that reminded me of things my inner child would love. I started putting stickers on everything, and each time I looked at them, I felt the spark of joy in my chest. It made me smile. I also started giving stickers to other adults in my life, and I've seen nothing but joy when they receive them too—I think there's something to it.

Every year since 2018, I have chosen a word for the year. (If this isn't something you have done before, or maybe you haven't done it in a while, I strongly recommend it!) Picking a word every year helps me to set my intention for what I want to do with that year and acts as a bit of a guidepost for me as I make decisions throughout that year. Over the years, I have made some pretty big impact on myself with these words:

Growth

Transform

Surrender

Impact

2025—HEAL

After the cards that 2024 had dealt me, I decided that 2025 was going to be the year I needed to lean more into the things that brought me joy, made me laugh, and made me smile. I needed to heal the parts of me that felt like they were drowning, and I was beginning to really understand for myself the POWER of laughter, play, and joy.

It's been so interesting to understand and realize that the answers to all the complex things in my life often live in the small, simple things that I, and most of our world, have gotten away from.

So in 2025, I did the most healing thing I could do and that's when I enrolled in **Pop Nation Canada**, a space where for 6 months I learned dances, sang songs, and did it just for FUN. And boy, did it come with a whole ton of laughter (and the self-trust story I told you earlier).

One of my favorite ways to laugh to this day, though, is watching funny videos. Mike will often find me laying in bed or on the couch busting a gut over videos of people falling, people being scared, or people doing silly things that end in them taking a tumble of some sort. I've now also started doing this to begin my days and have taken to sharing them on my social media to spread laughter to anyone who watches along. I can easily sit down for 5 to 10 minutes and reap all these benefits, and I do that so quickly. I also love to spread joy by forwarding funny reels to others for a laugh, too. Many of my friends are on the receiving end of these ridiculous videos that I can't get enough of often. But it's in this small practice, and some others I have shared with you in this chapter, that I have identified simple and easy ways to create feel good moments in my day. We all deserve those moments, very often, and more than we usually allow ourselves to.

When was the last time you belly laughed until your face hurt?

When was the last time you did something you used to do as a kid?

When was the last time you played, sang, danced, or even colored?

You should try it again. Your soul and the child inside of you are asking for it.

What would you hear if you listened to her?

CHAPTER 9

The [Afternoon] Delights of Life— This is NOT a Chapter About Gratitude

LISTENNNN, I went back and forth about whether I wanted to include something in the book about this topic. I think I hesitated mainly because gratitude feels overused. It's like sensationalized to where maybe for some of you it's become something that turns you off.

Find gratitude in the small things.

Enjoy the simple things in life.

These statements might drive you bonkers, and I don't blame you. They can sound like pie in the sky bogus advice when you're knee-deep while life is "life-ing" and you're just trying to juggle all the balls, raise the kids, wear all the hats, navigate work, and keep your head above water. You think to yourself, oh great, so now I have to feel gratitude, in the middle of all this mess? How? What? I don't think so. It can feel really disconnected from what your life actually feels like most days. Sometimes it might even feel like people use it to tell you to stop complaining or to look on the bright side while you're drowning. It can feel fake and like an impossible stretch. I wasn't sure if I wanted to even go there.

But then after more thought, I was like bro, I have to. Because for all the times gratitude feels hard to think about, or like something we *should feel* but don't, there's also the other side of that coin. The quiet, less showy but way more important side that in certain moments over the last 5 years have actually saved me. Not in a dramatic, *my whole life changed overnight* kinda way, but in a slow, barely notice-able-until-it-was kind of way. And if you don't want to call it a gratitude practice, you could also call it something else—you could be like Ross Gay and call it *finding the delights in life*. I loved the sound of finding the little delights.

Ross Gay is the author of *The Book of Delights*. This book is a collection of short, daily essays that he wrote over the course of a year, each reflecting on something whether it was big or small that brought him delights, which is also just a fancy way of saying he was finding gratitude in all of the moments of his life. These delights range from moments in nature, funny interactions with strangers, small acts of kindness, and nostalgic memories to simple pleasures like the taste of fresh fruit or the feel of sunshine on skin. (I will list some of MY favorite delights later!)

What makes it such a cool concept is the intention and the slowing down nature of the practice, and as we've already discussed in this book, it's often by the power of repetition that we are really able to create lasting and permanent shifts in our brains. Gay committed to noticing one delight every day and writing about it, which not only shifted his perspective toward joy and the lighter moments of life, but it also showed me how many delights we often overlook in our daily rush. Which is kinda what I want you to realize by reading this chapter! Finding the delights is everything—the afternoon delights!

That sounds weird right? There's a story there that I kinda feel like I have to share here because maybe it will make you laugh—a little glimmer of joy. (And also some insight as to why I named this chapter what I did!)

It was a sunny summer day one weekend, and I had spent most of the morning outside doing yard work, which is one of my favorite things to do. I often neglect inside work during the summer months because I like to be outside in the back-yard as often as I can. I relish in it because the Canadian winters are always coming back around, and if you live here, you get it. As I was outside working away, I thought it would be nice to catch up with my uncles on the back deck in the warm weather. I thought we could sun bathe, have a little cocktail, and enjoy each other's company, something we loved to do. My uncles and I are very close and exchanging invitations like this is pretty common for us. So, I opened up my phone and shot my one uncle a text message,

It's a super nice day out, want to come over for a little after-noon delight? We can sit out on the back deck.

Immediate response.

EWWWWWW, you're my niece! But hanging out sounds nice.

I was confused. In my mind, the song *sky rocket's in flight, afternoon delight* was playing, and it meant an afternoon drink, like a little yummy delight to break up the day ...

You do NOT know what afternoon delight means dear, he proceeded to tell me. So, I Googled it. Turns out afternoon delight, for most people, means a shag. Luckily, my uncles and I have good senses of humor; I just about died laughing ... and I never asked him to come over for an afternoon delight again.

Sitting outside with the sun on my face and a cold drink in my hand—delightful. **Grateful. Lifts the vibe.**

The second summer that my Eloise was on this earth, I decided I wanted the 3 of us to have a really fun summer, to make all the memories. Mike could only get select time off of work for our week holiday with his full-time work schedule, and because we had designed our lives that I was the primary caregiver at home, it meant that summer break was kind of my summer break from work too. Aside from our family tradition of going away to the cottage for a week, I thought it would be fun to go away somewhere, on a road trip to stay overnight, just us girls. At the time, my friend owned a B&B in the small town of Leamington, Ontario, which was about 3 hours south from us, and she had suggested we come and stay with her! We planned to spend some time just the 3 of us, but my friend also had daughters, so we made some plans to hangout with them as well. I knew it was going to be a great trip.

Planning to pack up the girls for a couple of days by myself was already a big deal, as I was still figuring out how this parenting 2 kids thing worked, but driving 3 hours in the car with them on the 401 ... a huge stretch. I was extra nervous when the weather for the day we drove down had a high chance of thunderstorms. Driving far distances had previously been something I really struggled with. There was this one time when I was in my early twenties that I drove to visit my cousin in Mississauga. We had a night out, and I stayed over, and in the morning when I woke up, I felt super anxious. We went out for some breakfast and the plan was that when breakfast was done I would get back in the car and drive the 50 minutes home. Sitting at the table, I kept having these waves of nausea, and I was certain I was going to be sick. This only made me spiral about the fact that I was going to have to make the drive home.

When we finished and headed back to her place, I wasn't feeling like I could make the drive home. My aunt ended up driving my car home, with me in it, and then my cousin followed in her car so that she could then bring her back to Mississauga. At the time, I just thought I was too hungover to drive, and that's what was causing the nauseous panicky feeling. But the more I thought about it, I was convinced I was too anxious thinking about driving back home because I needed to take the highway, and that's what caused me to not feel well and not be able to drive.

That's how bad my fear of driving could be.

There were multiple times over the 2 days that led up to my road trip with the girls where I had to talk myself out of canceling the trip. On the morning of, when the forecast hadn't changed much, I was a ball of nerves packing up the car. The excited energy from the girls was a distraction ... a distraction that I welcomed. I was grateful to have them and their innocent, happy energy. **Grateful. Vibe lifted a bit.**

A torrential downpour, so heavy that our windshield wipers couldn't keep up, hit us about an hour into the 3-hour drive. Not only that, but we were on a stretch of highway that was under construction, so the road was down to 2 extremely narrow lanes with barriers on both sides. There was nowhere for me to go. I turned off the music, and the car was quiet as I white knuckled forward. I thought to myself many times about whether I should turn back and say forget it, but I knew that if I turned around, I would also have to back track through all the weather I just drove through. "You can do this, Mommy," said Clara from the backseat. I was grateful for her at the moment, grateful for her intuition and the encouraging words she felt compelled to give me. **Grateful. Vibe lifted back up.**

Not more than 30 minutes down the road, the clouds cleared up, and for the rest of the drive, it got sunnier and sunnier. By the time we got to my friend's place, it was gorgeous, and she told me the pool was waiting for us. We dropped our things in our room, put on our swimsuits, and spent the rest of the afternoon lounging in the sun and swimming in the water. It was bliss, and I remember sitting on the side of the pool looking at the girls laughing together, thinking, "I am so grateful that I came. I'm so glad I pushed through that moment of BIG discomfort to get here. I'm so grateful I had them in the car with me." I took a quiet moment to anchor that in, a moment that I could have easily missed and instead I could have stayed in the anxiousness of the drive to getting there.

Gratitude doesn't have to be pretty or loud. It doesn't have to be shared in a caption on your IG feed or written in a fancy notebook, though I do love a good gratitude journaling session every now and again. You don't have to list 10 things you're grateful for every night before bed to prove it either. You just have to *notice* the good things. That's it. That's the whole thing. And noticing—even the tiniest thing—changes you. I truly believe it does. It's changed me.

It's easier now than it ever has been to catch myself in tough moments to find the good, or look for a lesson, or even when things are going well, to really stop and take a moment to soak it all in.

I think that sometimes practicing gratitude is somewhat misunderstood. We think that being grateful means pretending everything is okay and ignoring what's hard, what's painful, or doesn't feel good. But that's not what it is, not at all.

Before she entered grade 5, my daughter found out she was the only one that wasn't going to be in the same class with her core group of girlfriends. There were 4 girls who all requested to be with each other, and somehow she got slotted into a separate class. That sucked. I felt sad for her. I even cried (remember I am sensitive). I tried to pull myself together before telling her, but then she came looking for me in the house and busted me crying. She asked me what was wrong, so I told her, and she cried too. We sat there for a moment in the feeling of it and then I said to her, "There's a lesson in here somewhere kiddo, and we'll find it, but it's okay to feel sad about it too."

"I think that sometimes practicing gratitude is somewhat misunderstood. We think that being grateful means pretending everything is okay and ignoring what's hard, what's painful, or doesn't feel good. But that's not what it is, not at all."

Gratitude isn't pretending or ignoring that hard things aren't happening too. It's saying ...

This is hard, and I'm finding the things to be grateful for, anyway.

I feel heavy, and I'm still noticing this moment.

I'm not okay, and there's still something beautiful here.

You get to be in both. You don't have to choose. Duality is a very real and constant part of the human experience, and two things can be true, just like two feelings and emotions can be at the same time. Brené Brown calls this the paradox of life. Gratitude isn't about erasing what's wrong—it's about anchoring to what's STILL right.

Remember when I told you how our family went through that immense loss with the business in 2024? It was shit. It was heavy, it was hard, and at times, we were not okay. But there were also times throughout that year that focusing on what we were grateful for, what the silver linings were, were the ONLY things that helped us to get through.

The truth was that entrepreneurship wasn't easy either. We had spent many winters on a tight budget because when you work seasonally, there aren't pay cheques in the winter. There were some weeks where there wasn't enough money in the business to get paid, and that took a toll on our finances. Working for someone else meant that we had a full winter of pay cheques and no stress for the first time in 10 years. **Grateful.** We actually had benefits again, meaning our insurance covered dentist, massage, and chiropractor visits. **Grateful.** There were no longer late nights out on sales quotes, or spent designing, drawing, or writing up contracts. **Grateful.**

"Duality is a very real and constant part of the human experience, and two things can be true, just like two feelings and emotions can be at the same time."

What really sold me though was learning how this practice can actually affect our bodies and brains. Gratitude isn't just a vibe, it's a literal nervous system regulator. Scientists have studied it, and you know how much I love a good scientific back-up ... then you can't fight me on it. Like guys, it's real. When we practice gratitude consistently, our brains rewire. They notice good things more easily and become wired to seek beauty instead of clouds. We feel calmer. We become more resilient. Our hearts slow down. Our nervous system moves out of fight more and into rest mode. It's like telling your body, "You're safe now. You're okay to relax." Over time, we become less reactive, less overwhelmed, and more grounded.

Gratitude also raises your frequency and the overall vibration in the world. I know, that sounds woo—but I love me some woo. Everything is energy. Emotions carry energy and frequencies and have certain levels of attraction. Fear, shame, guilt—they're heavy ones. Gratitude? It's light. It opens your heart. It shifts the entire game. It's like adjusting your inner radio station for clarity, warmth, and alignment. When you're in a state of gratitude, even just for a second, you vibrate higher. You attract more ease. More grace. More synchronicity. And when you're in that state, your decisions, your conversations, your thoughts, who you do and don't allow into your energy (remember that chapter about your relationships with others?)—they all reflect that energy back.

I like practicing gratitude in ways that don't feel forced or showy and that feel good for me. When I first started my growth journey, every new thing that I learned I tried to incorporate it in my own life exactly the way I had learned I should, even if it felt sorta weird. The example coming to mind is lemon water with cayenne pepper and honey—do you remember that time? I had read somewhere it was great for your gut and great for your metabolism, both things I was wanting to work on. I would choke down that concoction every bloody day like it was my job even though I didn't really love it because someone told me I should. I especially hated the intense jolt of straight cayenne pepper at the bottom of the cup, but I suffered through that for almost a month, legit. Now, I just drink lemon water, and not all the time, only sometimes, because that feels good for me. And I save the cayenne pepper for my kale chips and chick peas- which usually have way too much cayenne on them too, I have a heavy hand. But that heavy hand feels good for me too, especially when the captain is involved.

Anyways, back to gratitude—I do it in a way that feels authentic to me. Like leaving random voice notes for friends and just saying, *Hey, I'm really grateful for you* or *I just wanted you to know I was thinking about you.* Or sitting at a red light and silently thinking of one moment that brought me peace that day. Or pausing before I eat and just noticing the smell of my food, or how warm my mug of coffee feels in my hands. These days, I often stop when I'm with the kids in the backyard, or when they are giggling together before bedtime. I take a mental snapshot and think about how grateful I am for those moments. That frequency keeps me amped for when challenging things happen, because they always do. The kids are usually smacking each other 5 minutes after the moment of gratitude ... imagine the vibe if my heart wasn't already pre-warmed.

"**Gratitude slows you down. It reminds you that life is happening right now, not after the next milestone or once everything is fixed.**"

These little things, when they become normal, start stacking. And before you know it, you're carrying this low-key sense of appreciation with you everywhere you go.

Gratitude makes you more present. When you're focused on what's missing or what went wrong or even what COULD go wrong, you're living in the past or future. But when you stop and say, Wow, *this moment right now is actually kind of beautiful*, you're here in the now. And in this culture of rushing and achieving and scrolling and comparing, that is everything. Gratitude slows you down. It reminds you that life is happening right now, not after the next milestone or once everything is fixed.

It deserves a small [big] place here, because being grateful has taught me life doesn't have to be extraordinary to be beautiful. It's on the regular days where you can find positivity and magic.

It's in the way the sky looks out our bedroom window when the sun is rising while I am making my bed first thing.

It's how your dog peeks her nose through the crack of the door when you're opening it to get home.

It's the breeze and the sun on your face.

It's in the way your bedsheets feel when you get into them at the end of the day, especially when it's washing day. Yes, I have been known to laugh, giggle, and squeal getting into my bed on many occasions just because!

It's the warm cup of coffee on the back deck or in your favorite couch spot.

It's the sunset, which honestly never gets old.

It's the sidewalk chalk on your front porch (even though sometimes it's messy).

It's not always obvious. But it's there. You may have to look for it and call it out to yourself or even those around you. Which gets really fun because you get to spread that joy with and influence others.

And when you start catching those moments, life feels less like something to survive and more like something to experience.

REFLECTION BLOCK

Gratitude Moment

What is one small thing today that brought you comfort, joy, or relief—and why are you grateful for it?

Do you feel that in your soul? That warmth, that's gratitude.

You don't have to become a gratitude guru, you just have to be open to looking around more. Notice the things that bring and feel like light, because there are often many. And maybe, when it feels right, you might even quietly say thank you to yourself or the world around you. Not because everything is perfect, but because, somehow, in the mess, you're still here, and it's still beautiful.

And that is enough to be grateful for. And it's also enough to make sure this chapter had a place here.

CHAPTER 10

Go TF Outside— The World Feels Better When You Step Into It

In the thick of the pandemic, when lock downs were in full effect, we were on what basically felt like house arrest. Work, school, relaxation, and play were all happening under the same roof, and it got to us all really quickly. At least it did for my household.

I was teaching for a private college part-time at the time, and my class had gone fully virtual. I had to be online every day from 7:30 am to 12:30 pm to teach my students and do teacher things. While we were online, they had to be my top priority, and they had my full attention, which meant anything that needed to be done with Clara and her schooling was done completely by Mike.

Mike was a carpenter by trade. He worked with tools and wood and numbers (it's a bit more complex than that, but I am just trying to paint a general picture here). He'd spent most of his days for the past almost 20 years with his head down, building with his hands, and keeping busy, and suddenly he was told he needed to stay home and not work. Not only that, but he is a very independent worker, and other than being onsite with his business partner, or sometimes having clients poke their heads in, he often worked quietly, alone, and that was something he enjoyed. Until he had to switch careers overnight; he now needed to be a kindergarten teacher.

Since I was teaching my own students virtually, and navigating the online teaching world with them, I was unavailable to help Clara get logged into her virtual classroom in the morning and keep her engaged in completing all the activities that were assigned by her teacher. The fact that we all went to online school, overnight, and were expected to just do it, still blows my mind. Like they took an entire system of operations for something that had been in person for decades, all the way from kindergarten to the adults I was teaching, and expected that everyone had a computer available, the knowledge to get that all up and running, the focus to be able to work independently, and the assumption that people didn't have other things going on at home. It was a lot for everyone, including my students.

My grown up students with kids and lives were having to get their kids ready, get their kids dropped off, manage their households while being expected to be present for class. When we were in person in the classrooms, they could physically come there and be away from all the distractions, but instead I had to expect them to be present and focused, all the while acknowledging how challenging it must have been to wear all the hats while simultaneously doing school. I didn't always agree with the way we/they had to live during that time, but life had to go on right? We had to do something because we didn't know how long it was going to go on for.

There are a lot of things and measures that happened during the pandemic here in Ontario, Canada, that I didn't agree with, but this really isn't the time to launder out that list. I will, however, say that expecting 5-year-olds to sit at a computer for the entire morning, focused and working on the activities assigned, expecting they are then going to hand in their work is a really tall order. I felt for these kids, but honestly I also felt for parents everywhere; if you had to do it you remember what it was like. If you have ever been around a child this age, then you might have noticed that getting them to sit still and focus on one task for a long period is a feat in itself. When you throw in, oh this happens at a computer where they need to stare at the screen or work on a paper, it's a recipe for disaster. Not to mention there is virtually no play or activity that can be done independently, so this meant that by default, parents who were at home working themselves also needed to be available to sit there with their kids while it happened.

We were fortunate enough that Mike literally could not "work from home" or "take it virtual" so he could be present with online schooling to help her through it, but going from a carpenter type of day and swapping to a kindergarten teacher/tutor 1:1 with a 5-year-old, throwing in the stress of the pandemic and the unknown—it was not the best parenting times of our lives, let's just say that.

Clara was a handful, with a lot of big emotions, understandably so. She didn't understand what was going on, why we were doing school on the computer, why she couldn't go to the school, why she couldn't see her friends, or her family … why anything was happening for that matter. And as a result, most of the time, she was pretty tough to wrangle to actually sit down and complete the activities. The teacher, aka Mr. Mike Mondoux, was doing his absolute best, but I am sure as someone who was battling the stress of the pandemic and being thrown into something like teaching, he was also navigating his own feelings and reactions about that. I think we all were, and during that time, I also don't think we gave ourselves enough grace with all the things that were expected of us to pivot. Often when I would come downstairs on break from teaching there would be some tension, and by the time I was wrapping up my day, the two of them were almost ready to break.

We needed some place to blow off steam, to reset, to get out of the house, and there was nowhere to go, except nature. They couldn't take nature away from us.

How We Made It Through

I remember this one particular winter day; it was pretty snowy and gloomy, but I was determined to get outside after both of our days were done. Trying desperately to cope with this season of our lives, I had quickly turned to spending the first hour after we were all done school taking Clara out of the house to 1 of the 2 trails near our house. Both trails we'd been on several times before, but they were quickly becoming our sanctuary and our place to find peace.

This particular day that I remember, it was a CHORE getting Clara dressed to go outside. Getting a young child to fully dress for the winter weather is kind of like trying to negotiate with an alligator to get them into a cage when they are already mad. The snow pants didn't feel right so she didn't want to wear them. The scarf and the hat were too scratchy, so she said she would be fine without them (in the snowstorm) and her boots were too heavy to wear. She did NOT want to go walking, but I was not taking no as an answer.

I buckled her into the car seat while tears were running down her face and I could feel myself getting more and more aggravated. I was trying to do something that I knew was going to make us all feel better, and it was so much harder than it needed to be. Life with a young child sometimes, am I right? Once we got to the trail, there weren't many cars in the parking lot. The government had closed the parks, deeming them to be unsafe to use, but they would not take away the trails. Many times we would pass tons of other people, using the trails for the same things I expect we were, too. Normalcy. Getting out of the house, and as a small way of keeping connected with others.

We started walking, and the wind was definitely colder than I thought it was going to be. I thought to myself in my head, *She's going to be complaining about this really soon.* But surprisingly, as we forged on, she didn't.

Because of the temperature, there weren't many people on the trail that afternoon, so we could hear the wind in the tree tops above us. The trail was nestled down a hill in a forest—trees lined the path on both sides, so all you could see were trees. This forest sheltered us from the cold wind. We weren't talking at this point, so as we continued along and I looked around at the trees, I could hear the snow crunching beneath our feet, the whooshing sound of our snow pants rubbing together, and the sniffling of our noses running from the cold. It was still and peaceful all around us.

I took a few deep breaths in through my nose, feeling the tingle of that cool air tickling my nose. I breathed it deep into the depths of my lungs.

in and out

in and out

in and out

I felt a wave of calm wash over me, and I encouraged Clara to do the same. I encouraged her to be present and out of her head. As we got farther down the trail, we got to a part that was lined with hills on both sides. She loved to climb up the sides of the hill as we walked the path and come down the other side, so I was waiting for her to take off in laughter, but she didn't. She just stopped.

"What's up, babe?" I asked her.

"Can I slide down this hill on my butt mommy?" she asked me in her little voice. (I still remember it like I heard it yesterday.)

"Sure babe, just be careful."

As she prepared to slide down the hill, I could see the joy bubbling up inside her. And as she made her way from the top to the bottom, she let out a squeal of glee.

"I want to do that again! Mommy, do you want to do it with me?"

For the next 15 minutes, we walked up that hill and came sliding back down in our snow pants. The fabric on the pants made them slippery like toboggans, so we were getting some speed. I laughed, she laughed. I shrieked, she shrieked. We rode together, snuggling the whole way down, and we also went down on our own. She insisted on doing it alone, showing me how proud she was going down head first. We were so present and in the moment that by the time we were done, the aggravation and the stress of the morning were gone. Blown away like the wind in the trees above us.

We hiked for longer that day. She had plenty to tell me about her morning school projects after her escapades on the hill. We talked about the bedroom layout from a "bird's eye view" they had to draw. She told me what a bird's eye view meant. Suddenly, the stressful feelings of the morning morphed into excitement and it was like they never existed, all because of being outside.

Nature heals. Period.

REFLECTION BLOCK

Nature Connection Exercise

The next time you step into a natural space slow down and engage your 5 senses. Notice what you can see, hear, feel, smell, and even taste in the air. Stay present with each sense for a few breaths. Afterward, write down what you noticed and how your body or emotions shifted.

"We were so present and in the moment that by the time we were done, the aggravation and the stress of the morning were gone. Blown away like the wind in the trees above us."

My connection with nature really grew during this time, and as much as the pandemic was such a challenging time for so many of us in so many ways, this reminder of the power of nature was opened up to me and has stuck with me ever since.

To support this chapter, I was researching the healing benefits of nature, because I know there is so much healing power to this free resource. I interestingly came across an article written by a doctor who shared that he actually prescribes nature to his patients to cope with the challenges of life and to manage their mental well-being.

Benefits of Spending Time Outdoors

According to research, being outside can lower blood pressure, heart rate, and stress; improve mood and immune function; allow for better sleep; and it can increase creativity. There are surprising social benefits, too. During early forest bathing experiments, physician Qing Li found that after a couple hours in the woods, blood pressure went down an average of 5 points. The effects didn't end once people left the trees either! Research showed that their stress hormones were measurably lower for a week. After forest bathing for 2 hours, 3 days in a row, markers of immune health showed improvement that lasted a week. And, of course, almost all the people said they just felt better, too![18]

We are primarily visual beings, so it is not surprising that just looking at beautiful natural scenes makes us feel good too. A heart surgeon at Vanderbilt suspected it did more than that. Looking at it closely, he found that his patients whose hospital room faced the forest healed faster than those who faced the parking garage. WHAT![19]

This was just one of the many articles that have been published that support why nature is so good for us on a psychological and cellular level. I didn't even fully realize the power of being outside until it was the only thing we had at our disposal for healing. Sounds about right though, doesn't it?

How You Can Use the Outdoors

Like I said earlier in this book, it often takes a huge event or milestone to happen in order for us to really lean into the things that fill our souls, to slow down, and to remember to tune back into the simple pleasures and joys that bring us bliss. We are mammals and historically, mammals lived outside y'all. For centuries, we spent so much time in nature. We slept, we lived, we walked, we laughed, and we spent slow moments in nature, appreciating its beauty and how it showed up for us and delivered us healing, every day.

But shit's really different now.

We see the sunshine but only through our windshields as we drive into our place of work. We feel the breeze on our faces but only as we are walking from the car into the building where we spend 8 hours only to turn around and go home and do it all again. We buy gym memberships to indoor places so we can get movement to try to take care of our body's primal needs to move. We buy all the expensive things to heal ourselves, and we work like crazy just to spend one week during the summer by water.

Okay, maybe I am exaggerating a bit—or maybe I'm not.

When was the last time you took your morning coffee onto the deck, or onto the porch, or the balcony? You took it out there and then you simply sat there. Maybe with your eyes closed and your face tilted upwards to feel the warmth of the sun, or you felt the crisp air on your face and you held a warm sweater up to your body? I am getting all the feelings, even writing that. Do you know what the morning dew smells like?

When was the last time you took yourself on a walk through the forest and really looked around? Felt the ground beneath your feet, looked at the surrounding trees, listened to the birds, the wind—nature. Just bathed in it.

Have you even heard of forest-bathing? It's a real thing!

Originating in Japan in the 1980, forest bathing, or *shin-rin-yoku*, is the Japanese practice of immersing yourself in nature to improve well-being. It's not about hiking or exercising, but about slowing down, engaging your senses, and mindfully connecting with the natural world around you. By simply walking through the forest, breathing deeply, and noticing the sights, sounds, and scents of nature, you can reduce stress, boost mood, and restore mental clarity. It's a gentle reminder to unplug and let nature do the healing.[20] So, this doesn't mean taking your marathon training into the forest, or walking and talking with someone, or listening to music in your air pods, but slowing down and immersing yourself in your surroundings.

As I walk, I love hearing leaves crinkling or snow crunching under my feet. I love hearing the birds chirping in the trees—you can even feed the chickadees in the forest near us so we always have birdseed in our car. I love feeling the wind against my cheeks, or that electric feeling that runs through my body when I return to my car, my cheeks flushed and sweaty from a winter hike.

Nature literally has the magical powers to change and lift your mood! It helps you to lean into your creativity and clears your mind to help you solve all your life problems. Okay, that's extreme, but I know this: while going outside won't solve all problems, it never made a situation worse. Outdoor time typically makes things better.

Are you someone who swears that water speaks to your soul? Me too.

In the warmer months, and the colder ones too at that, I live for being by a body of water. (Counting down the hours to head away for a cottage weekend as I type this to you right now!) This has always been something that I've felt inside me, even before I really connected with how much nature means to me.

When I was a teenager, we had a cottage on Lake Erie in Long Point. Every single time we drove down there, as we got closer to the lake, I would literally have a visceral reaction. I would get giddy, excited inside. I could barely contain it. When my eyes caught a sight of the water, my heart would flutter. Not even exaggerating, it still does! And in fact, if you ask Mike, he will tell you that pretty much every time I see water I say, "Oh, *there it is!*"

As soon as we parked and unloaded everything into the cottage, the first place I would head was the water or the beach. With my swimsuit on, no matter how cold it was, I would be in there, cleansing and resetting, though I didn't have the language to name it as that at the time. It was a running joke with my family that I would always be the first one of the season to brave the cold water every May 2-4 long weekend, if not earlier. After a night of drinking, when I wasn't feeling too great, my first instincts would tell me, *Get in the water, you will feel better.* And it always worked. Submerging my body dulled or numbed any headache or nausea. To this day, if I am feeling off, I will try to get into the water, even if it just means I take a shower to reset myself.

More recently, I have been exploring cold water therapy and hydrotherapy. I talk about how amazing water and nature are so much that even my kids know that water can heal you if you are not feeling well, both physically or emotionally. In fact, if they are having a meltdown, or I can tell that they are over-tired, I will force them to take a shower. Without fail, after a few minutes of being there, the crying usually turns into humming in the shower, or they are simply quiet, but I can feel the sense of calm in them.

REFLECTION BLOCK
Micro-Moments of Nature Action Step

Commit to one small, way you can invite nature into your routine this week. Write down the moment you'll choose each day, and at the end of the week, reflect on how it impacted your mood, or energy.

"Nature literally has the magical powers to change and lift your mood! It helps you to lean into your creativity and clears your mind to help you solve all your life problems."

A few years ago, I hosted a full moon event at a local indoor sauna and water therapy place near me. I wanted to host it there in particular because not only was it different from anything I had ever hosted, but I wanted the participants to experience cold and sauna therapy if they had never dabbled in it before.

After doing a journaling exercise where you had to write the things you were ready to release, we followed it up with a physical cleansing of our energy. This sauna had a cold plunge tub, where you submerged yourself in water, but they also had a cold pull bucket. Essentially, it was an elevated bucket of cold water that when you stood underneath it and pulled the string, it would dump the freezing water on your head.

The intention with this ritual was to cleanse and literally wash away the things that were no longer serving you. As each person lined up, stood with their eyes closed, and pulled the water onto their heads, I could hear the buzz in the room. The energy shifted.

One participant came up to me and told me she was a little apprehensive about coming. She shared with me that she had never heard of "any of this stuff" but she really enjoyed the messages I shared in my business so she decided to try it out.

If I hadn't been here tonight, I never would have believed the difference you can feel with a simple bucket of water.

She shared she had been struggling with her mental health and that her mind had felt foggy for the last two weeks.

Andrea, I don't know if it's your energy or if it really was this water ritual, but I feel different.

She followed up with me weeks later and stated that things really had made a shift for her. She thanked me again for opening up her eyes to a tool that she had never considered before. It was a pretty special moment for me to have been able to share that with her.

There are so many tools and resources available to us that are separate from the advances and complexities of modern medicine. There is definitely a time and a place for these advances, but I also want to remind you there are simple alternatives out there for what we need as biological human beings, we just have to be open and lean in.

CONCLUSION

The End

Here we are, at the end of this book—you made it, you're cured, hooray!

All of the years and decades of programming you've had that we worked through and discussed will never come up for you again!

Okay, I hope you know that I'm kidding. You probably do.

I'm so honored you took this wild journey with me. I will never forget that you bought this book and spent your valuable time reading it with me. Regardless of how many times this happens, it is such an honor. You are so special and so worth it, and the people in your life are really lucky to have you around (I wish I could give you a hug right now. I've been told I give the best ones). I hope you're **grateful** to yourself too, because by now I sure hope you've learned and maybe even embodied the power of being your own best friend, of telling yourself "good job," and being proud of yourself. It matters. And I know, in your life, with how busy it can be sometimes, it's not always easy to prioritize yourself when you're juggling all the roles, and all the hats, and all the expectations. Give yourself a pat on the back for taking the time to read this book from cover to cover. I always feel so good when I finish reading a book.

"Learning is living! It's a lifelong unfolding, a constant practice, an ongoing severely ungraceful choreographed dance between what we know, what we feel, what we desire, what's not working, what we no longer want or need, what we are ready to embrace, and what we are ready to release."

But to circle back about being done and at the end, I want to remind you that really, there is no "end" to this kind of work. This growth journey to break free from the shoulds and to move into more joy, the learning, the growing, the growing … it's not a one-and-done deal. Could you imagine, though? Picking up a book that solves all your life's problems and changes things forever overnight? That's a pipe dream and honestlyyyyy, would kinda take the fun out of it. Learning is living! It's a lifelong unfolding, a constant practice, an ongoing severely ungraceful choreographed dance between what we know, what we feel, what we desire, what's not working, what we no longer want or need, what we are ready to embrace, and what we are ready to release.

We've talked about sooo much in these pages and these chapters, haven't we? Such good chats.

I poured out my heart and soul out to you, do you feel it? I sure hope you do (maybe you even said, yep, in your head!). We dove into the importance of thought work—those sneaky little stories we carry around, stories that aren't even ours half the time, and usually without even realizing it and without knowing how much power they hold over us. We explored boundaries, the ones we set for ourselves and the ones we navigate in our relationships with others, which as we know, are both equally important to consider! We talked about the ways we show up for ourselves and how cool it can be to put ourselves first … also that it's completely okay to do so, and, in fact, I highly encourage it! The juicy topic of self-trust—I hope you are all the way in on that one! We explored the ways we care for our bodies and minds, and how laughter, play, and time in nature aren't just nice little extras but essential ingredients to a life well-lived. (Go finish this book outside if you aren't already there!) And now, as you close this book, I want you to remember one thing above all else.

Let's take a moment to breathe together, shall we? I don't know about you, but sometimes when I get near the end of the chapter or the end of the book, I get excited, and I read a little faster, so I can get there. But I don't want this intentional time to end too quickly. So let's take a breath.

Read this first and then do the following:

Close your eyes.

While your eyes are closed, rest your hands on your heart and take 3 really deep breaths. In through the nose ... fill all the way up. Hold it a second, and then out through the mouth (or nose again), emptying completely. **Go.**

Okay, good—now back to the things that you're remembering above all else—no pressure.

I want to leave you with the 3 fundamentals of the work that I do with my 1:1 and group clients and the way I encourage us all to show up for ourselves with. I want you to remember **grace, compassion, and acceptance.**

For yourself. For your journey. For your season of life, whatever that may be. For the lessons you've learned, both the ones that felt good and the ones that really fucking hurt, the ones you're still learning, and even the ones you keep having to learn repeatedly (because let's be real, some things just take time to sink in).

"The beauty of this journey isn't in reaching for some final destination. When you can truly integrate that knowing into your soul, it changes everything. Instead of racing for the finish line, it's learning to be present with yourself, no matter where you are."

There is no magical moment where you wake up one day and think, *Ah, I've finally made it! Bliss unlocked, joy on autopilot, all problems resolved.* That's just not how this whole human experience works. Life will always ebb and flow, and as long as you are a human, there will always be things that come your way that you won't be able to expect.

Some seasons will feel light and expansive depending on what is going on in your life and the lives of those that you love around you, and others will feel heavy and hard, like you can't seem to get ahead. On those days, you might feel longing for the habits and mindset that you know served you well before. Some days you'll wake up ready to conquer the world and others you'll just want to crawl back under the covers and pretend the world doesn't exist. It's all okay, and it's all normal. The pendulum will always continue to swing, move, and shift ... the moon always comes through its faded darkness phase back into whole again—and so do you.

The beauty of this journey isn't in reaching for some final destination. When you can truly integrate that knowing into your soul, it changes everything. Instead of racing for the finish line, it's learning to be present with yourself, no matter where you are. It's meeting yourself with kindness, even when you feel stuck, overwhelmed, or like you've taken 10 steps backward. Remember, like you would for your best friend, right?

If you take nothing else from this book (though, selfishly, I hope you take A LOT), let it be this: **you are allowed to be human.** You are allowed to have bad days. You are allowed to struggle. You are allowed to feel frustrated, lost, or uncertain. You are allowed to change your mind, to pivot, to outgrow things that once felt right, or politely release the things that no longer serve you. Jobs, places, habits, mindsets, people. You are allowed to pursue joy just because it feels good, not because it's productive or "useful." You are allowed to be a messy, evolving, ever-learning human.

I hope you carry with you the ability to practice self-compassion. Part of honoring and building that relationship with yourself is understanding it's not about being perfect, doing everything right, or having all the answers. It's about being gentle with yourself in the same way you would with a close friend. Let's bring that back again … how would you speak to someone you love when they're struggling? Would you say, *Ugh, you're such a failure. Why can't you just get it together?* No! You'd say, *Hey, it's okay. You're doing your best. Having hard days—having hard days is allowed.*

How you speak to yourself is important. The way you hold yourself through hard moments matters. The way you choose to soften instead of shame, to encourage instead of criticize, to nurture instead of neglect … all of it matters.

The idea that personal growth is an ever-evolving and growing process isn't just something nice to believe in … remember, it's backed by science! Studies have shown that engaging in continuous self-reflection, emotional regulation, and mindfulness practices leads to greater overall well-being. It's so cool that this work is being explored now. What a gift for our kids and for future generations to have this information. It's also a gift to know that it's never too late.

Dr. Carol Dweck's Stanford University research showed that people can improve their skills and intelligence through learning and hard work. Also known as a "growth mindset." A growth mindset is **the belief that abilities and intelligence can be developed through dedication, effort, and learning from experiences, especially setbacks.** It emphasizes that intelligence is not a fixed trait but can be improved through learning and persistence. Her research found that individuals who adopt a growth mindset experience lower levels of stress, higher motivation, and overall increased life satisfaction. This is because they view challenges as opportunities rather than as threats, and additionally have more tools and perspectives to cope when things get challenging.[21]

More research from the field of positive psychology, pioneered by Dr. Martin Seligman, showed that individuals who regularly engage in gratitude practices, self-compassion, and cognitive reframing experience greater resilience, lower levels of anxiety and depression, and a stronger sense of purpose.[22]

What does this mean? It means that continuing to challenge your thoughts, cultivate joy, set boundaries, and engage in self-reflection isn't just a nice idea—it's a scientifically backed way to improve your life.

Joy isn't just something that magically appears in your life when you've "fixed" everything girlfriend, it's something you cultivate. It's something you practice, even on the days when it feels impossible. Find the tiny moments. The first sip of coffee in the morning. The way the sunlight hits your face. That deep belly laugh you share with a friend. Those funny videos you find on the internet. The ridiculous amazon reviews. A hug from someone you love. These are the things that make life rich. These are the things that remind us why we're here. I know life gets busy and the responsibilities pile up. It's easy to ignore your happiness when you are busy dealing with other things. I lived it in 2023, and I learned the hard way. Hear me when I say that joy is not a reward for when everything is done it's something you deserve now, through all of it.

So, where do you go from here?

You keep going forward.

You consistently show up for yourself.

Keep challenging the narratives that don't benefit you.

Read this book again if you need it. Download the audio integrations to keep the rewiring and repetition happening. Keep setting boundaries that protect your peace. Keep choosing joy, even when it feels small. Remind yourself that you're a work in progress, not a problem to be solved. Intentionally and actively free yourself from the shoulds. Life is meant to be lived, not just managed. You are worthy of love, rest, play, and ease and not because you've earned it, but simply because you exist.

And on the days when you forget? When it all feels too hard... When old habits creep back in ...

Come back to grace. Come back to compassion. Come back to yourself.

Because no matter where you are, no matter how many times you stumble, you are always, always worthy of getting up, moving forward and living a life filled with bliss.

I care about you so freaking much.

Let's Make It Stick— Download Your Audio Integrations!

Reading this book is one thing—but living it? That's where the real magic happens.

I've created something extra for you: quick visualizations and simple activations to go with each chapter. They're here to help you integrate what you've just read and keep doing the work in a way that actually fits into your life. Whether you lay down and listen to them, send them through your car while you drive, or listen to them into your earbuds while you walk, these are designed to help you further integrate the lessons and the learnings from this book to help you truly embody bliss in your life.

You can scan the QR code at the end of each chapter to access them or visit the listed web link to download the folder— they're easy to use and designed to support you as you keep growing.

Come back to them whenever you need. This work gets deeper every time you do it.

Access your FREE audio integrations and be inspired to take action!

Acknowledgements

Let's be real here, I stared at this page for a while, because to me, acknowledgments are hard to write.

They're not hard to write because I don't know who to thank, but because *everyone* in my life touches this very human work in some way, because as I change, the work and the impact changes. And I change as a result of what I learn from my community. Every conversation, every late-night talk, every road trip therapy session, every shared laugh or breakdown, it all shapes who I am and what I create.

This book didn't come together in isolation. I started the outline of this book in April 2023 when I was heading to Vegas for a conference, and finally sat down to start it in Aug 2023. This book was written in the in-between moments of my real life that I share here with you. Every person in my orbit informs my reality, and this book is a reflection of that shared energy you've given me, both in gifts and in lessons. I feel so honored to share time and space with some pretty impactful people.

To my husband: thank you for being such a big believer and supporter. Over the years as I've grown, my yearning for more in many aspects has been challenging I'm sure. But I regularly am met with you holding space for all my ideas and my evolution. Your grounded love has been the foundation that's allowed me to rise again and again.

To my girls: I saw a quote that read, "*Your kids will either inherit your trauma or your transformation. Choose wisely, because you will transmit what you do not transform*", and it feels like everything. You are my why, you know, my mirror, and my reminder of what's possible when we listen to the lessons that can come from the kids in our lives. As much as I am teaching you about the world and how to be within it, you teach me more than you'll ever know. Watching you grow into your own power, in your own unique ways gives me the drive to keep stepping into mine. You make me want to be the kind of woman I hope you'll become.

My editor Anya, you have been such a cheerleader for me and really helped me to develop this story into what it is. Thank you for your humor, your candor, and your willingness to make this book great with me.

Courtney, and LeadHer Publishing—you KNOW I couldn't have done this, in this way, without you. My girl, thank you.

To my BLOOM ladies: you are proof of what happens when women fully see you, honor you, and give space for all parts of you. You inspire me endlessly.

To all the women who have touched, challenged, or changed my life, thank you for showing me what strength looks like in all its forms. As I sit here writing this and think about each of you individually, I can't even begin to believe the circle of womanhood I feel so lucky to have attracted. Every one of you has left a mark on my heart and in my story. You've each been a part of this creation in your own way, and as you read this, maybe you found yourself in my story.

And to you, the reader—thank you for saying yes to yourself by being here. For choosing growth, for opening your heart, and for walking this path alongside me. You are not just reading these words—you are *becoming* them.

This one's for all of us. The women who rise, rewrite, and remember our power over and over again.

About The Author

Andrea Mondoux

@the.balance.bliss
andrea@thebalancebliss.ca
www.thebalancebliss.ca

Photo by Click Photography

Andrea Mondoux is a Transformation Coach, Speaker, and 7x published author who's made it her mission to help women rewrite their stories and rise into the most unapologetic, fulfilled versions of themselves. With her signature blend of honesty, humor, and heart, Andrea keeps it real about what it actually takes to grow—not the perfectly curated kind of growth, but the "I'm doing my best and figuring it out as I go" kind.

A former front line social service worker and Community Service Worker instructor, she blends her social work knowledge, her lived experience, and her coaching certification to support and transform her clients.

Through her coaching, retreats, and writing, Andrea empowers women to stop waiting for the perfect moment and start showing up as the woman they're becoming—today. Her work blends mindset, self-trust, and radical self-compassion, reminding every woman that she's capable of more than she's been giving herself credit for.

When she's not leading transformative conversations or hosting events that spark deep connections, you can find Andrea laughing with her family, sipping a strong coffee, and finding joy in life's everyday moments—the messy, beautiful ones that make it all real.

You can learn more about her and the work she does at thebalancebliss.ca or follow along her real life moments at @the.balance.bliss on Instagram.

Endnotes

1   Madeline Miles, "Are You Reaching Your Full Potential? A Guide to Personal Development," *BetterUp Blog*, February 10, 2022

2   Saul McLeod, "Maslow's Hierarchy of Needs," *Simply Psychology*, accessed November 14, 2025

3   Don Miguel Ruiz, "The Four Agreements," *miguelruiz.com*, n.d., accessed November 3, 2025

4   Noah St. John, "Why Your Mind Is Like an Instagram Feed," *HuffPost*, November 26, 2014

5   Crystal Raypole, "How Many Thoughts Do You Have Each Day? And Other FAQs," *Healthline*, February 28, 2022

6   Matt Puderbaugh and Prabhu D. Emmady, "Neuroplasticity," in *StatPearls [Internet]* (Treasure Island (FL): StatPearls Publishing, updated May 1, 2023), accessed November 3, 2025

7   Darius Cikanavicius, "The Trap of External Validation for Self-Esteem," *Psych Central*, August 28, 2017

8   Eshal Fatima, "The Power of Self-Validation: You Are Successful Only When You Give Yourself the First Pat," *Medium* (Write A Catalyst), January 2024

9   Harvard Health Publishing, "Understanding the Stress Response," *Harvard Health*, April 3, 2024

10   NeuroLaunch Editorial Team, "Chronic Stress and Mental Health: An AP Psychology Perspective," *NeuroLaunch*, August 18, 2024

11   Linda Bloom and Charlie Bloom, "Self-Trust and How to Build It," *Psychology Today* (blog: Stronger at the Broken Places), September 12, 2019

12   Neil A. Rector, Danielle Bourdeau, Kate Kitchen, Linda Joseph-Massiah, and Judith M. Laposa, An Information Guide: Anxiety Disorders (Toronto: *Centre for Addiction & Mental Health*, 2024), accessed November 3 2025

13   Claudia M. Elsig, "The Dangers of Suppressing Emotions," *The CALDA Clinic*, accessed November 3, 2025

14   Crystal I. Lee, "Boundaries 101: What Are Boundaries?," *L.A. Concierge Psychologist*, May 21, 2022

15   Pamela Gerloff, "You're Not Laughing Enough, and That's No Joke," *Psychology Today* (blog: The Possibility Paradigm), June 21, 2011

16   Lawrence Robinson, Melinda Smith, and Jeanne Segal, "Laughter Is the Best Medicine," *HelpGuide.org*, May 16, 2025

17   Thomas Verny, "The Science Behind Why Laughter Can Help You Live Life to the Fullest," *The Globe & Mail*, May 9, 2024

18   Leif Hass, "How Nature Helps Us Heal," *Greater Good* (UC Berkeley), October 25, 2021

19   Leif Hass, "How Nature Helps Us Heal," *Greater Good* (UC Berkeley), October 21, 2021

20   Qing Li, "'Forest Bathing' Is Great for Your Health. Here's How to Do It," TIME, May 1 2018

21   Growth Mindset and Enhanced Learning," Teaching Commons, *Stanford University*, accessed November 4, 2025

22   Melissa Madeson, Ph.D., "The PERMA Model: Your Scientific Theory of Happiness," *PositivePsychology.com*, February 24, 2017